13628 Budget 75

john w. cataldo

Lettering

a guide for teachers

davis publications inc. / worcester / massachusetts

12 11 10 9 8

cover calligraphy by gail miller

FOREWORD

because basic letter forms are more-or-less fixed by precedent and tradition, one could rationalize that there is little opportunity in lettering for aesthetic expression and personal interpretation. yet, a study of the work of our best calligraphers and type designers gives ample evidence that there is considerable area of prerogative where the artist may leave the stamp of his own personality and purpose. this book, sensitively designed by the author, proves this point. we too often see students transfer letter forms verbatim from alphabets and type specimens to otherwise original designs and layouts, without any apparent personal involvement in the design of the lettering. the author rightly recognizes the fact that self-identification as well as facility in lettering stems from a direct use of the tool which helps fashion the form, rather than from merely filling in outlines borrowed from another. throughout, the emphasis is on developing design quality leading to further experiments in individual interpretation. because this approach is fundamental, the book provides a good foundation for individuals and classes on both the secondary and advanced levels.

john w. cataldo is a versatile artist and a stimulating teacher. during his undergraduate days at the massachusetts school of art, he conducted a significant study in lettering with a saturday high school class. he later studied calligraphy with arnold bank at columbia university, and graphics design with john paul jones at the university of california at los angeles. he has taught lettering and design at the university of missouri, the new york state university college for teachers at buffalo, and at teachers college, columbia university. the meticulous devotion he gave to the preparation of this book is his own best introduction.

d. k. winebrenner

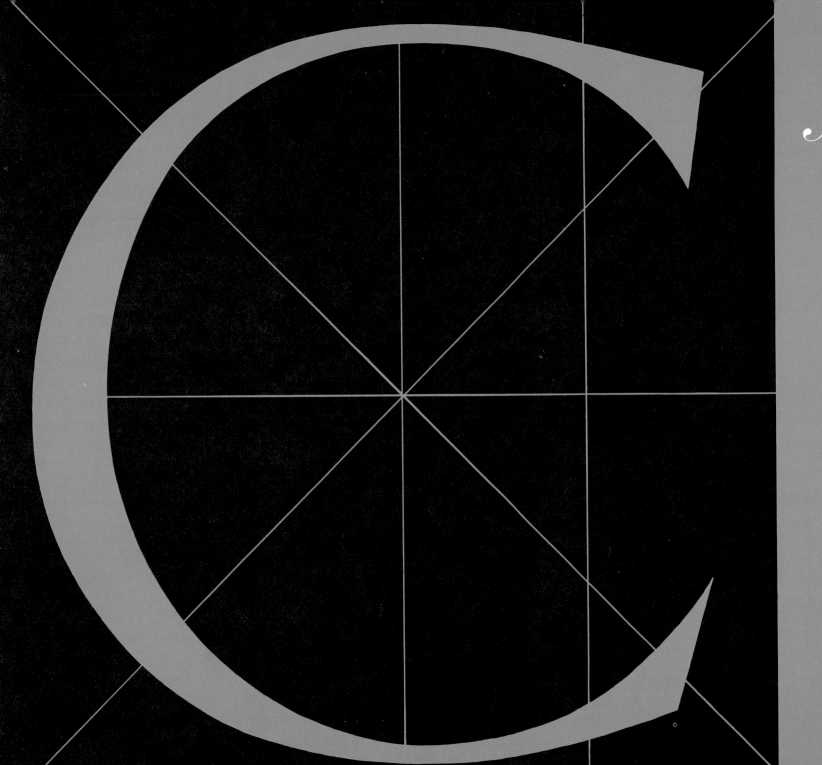

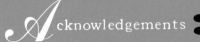cknowledgements

m.a.

e. j.

e. a cataldo

l. a.

b. a.

g. e.

r. & a.

d. k. winebrenner

jack arends

s. a. czurles

priscilla nye

r. l. bertoll

don nichols

c. mc waid

t. mc sherry

charles pollock

c. e. bauer

g. yee

s. plum

students and friends

the characters of our alphabet were 'derived from primitive realities and conceptualized into visual equivalents. forms of notation, image and symbol-making were in use over 135,000 years ago in ritual and ceremonial acts. then, as now, they provided a binding and reassuring medium for preserving communities of similar interests and concerns. a medium that made primitive human existence tolerable.

images preceded words by centuries and that same energy and sensory vitality that is reflected in root images (such as those found in the cuevas de altamira) still inherits the twenty-six phonetic signals of our western alphabet. for the first images were painted and sung, and those visual and oral impulses provided a common basis for the development of languages. every tribe, every culture, derived its preferred images from a similar root source of natural phenomena and cosmic experiences. the force and impact of language forms is derived from this first sensory and sensuous transaction between people, universal phenomena and the urgent need for human beings to express and communicate with each other.

j.w.c. 1974

to express himself, the student eventually has to control the symbols of his culture. lettering is symbolism; it forms a language and it has to do with meanings. the forms herein included, like natural selection, are the ones that persisted throughout centuries. they have in a sense proven themselves; they are the symbols that human beings prefer to use.

j.w.c. 1966

contents

felt pen lettering by b. arseneau

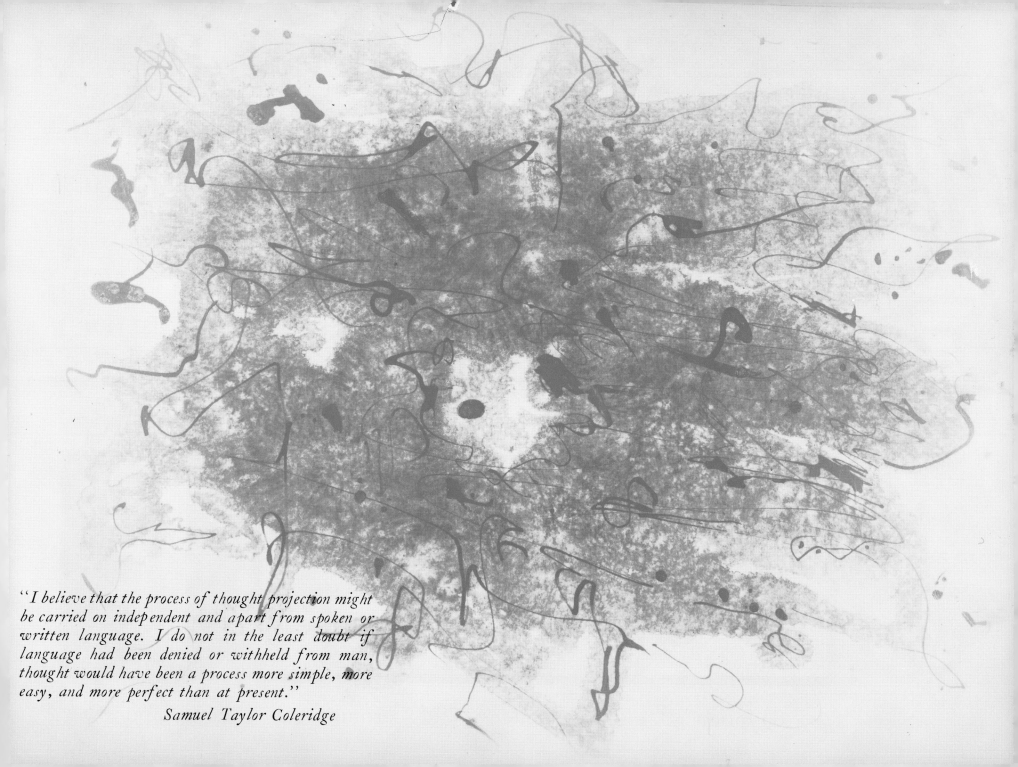

"I believe that the process of thought projection might be carried on independent and apart from spoken or written language. I do not in the least doubt if language had been denied or withheld from man, thought would have been a process more simple, more easy, and more perfect than at present."

Samuel Taylor Coleridge

F O R M

the stages of man's cultural development are evidenced by the growth of his communication symbols.

primitive thought projection through a graphic representation.

symbol evolution

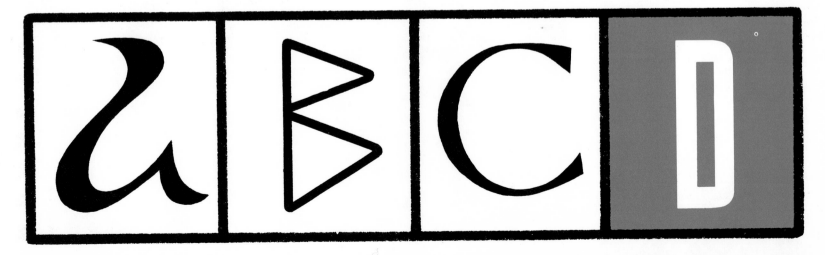

egyptian   hellenic   roman   contemporary

CAPITALIS

the capitalis letter form of the ancient romans was the prototype for our contemporary letters; very few changes have been made from this original, precise form.

lettering /

the calligrapher can adjust the size and the shape of each letter in the word, or adjust any word to make the line visually more pleasing. the typographer cannot make the same changes as quickly or as effectively.

typography /

type uses a different measure; it is more mechanical and depends on mechanical processes.

d d d

the precise character of the machine, together with space and time saving demands, led to the development of sans serif alphabets.

early type was the imitative product of existing writing forms.

CE

thought projection has been and will continue to be directly related to and limited by the formative character of the medium used. the pen, brush, and chisel shaped the peculiar form of the graphic symbol. thought projection is in a process of continual adaptation to the communication needs of mankind and will adapt itself to the period it functions in.

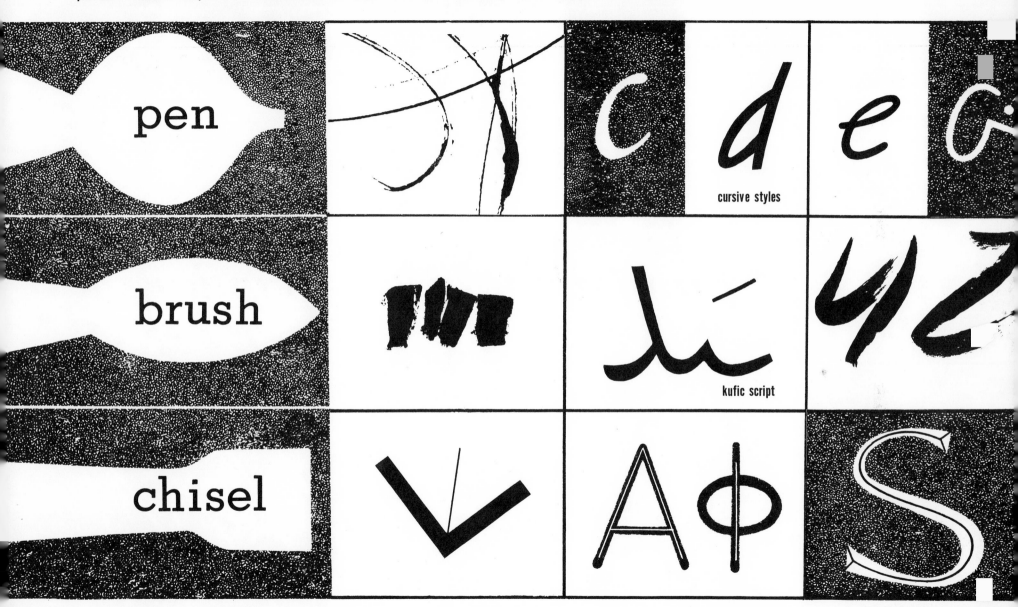

pen

brush

chisel

cursive styles

kufic script

greek archaic

roman inscription

line

and its' inherent significance

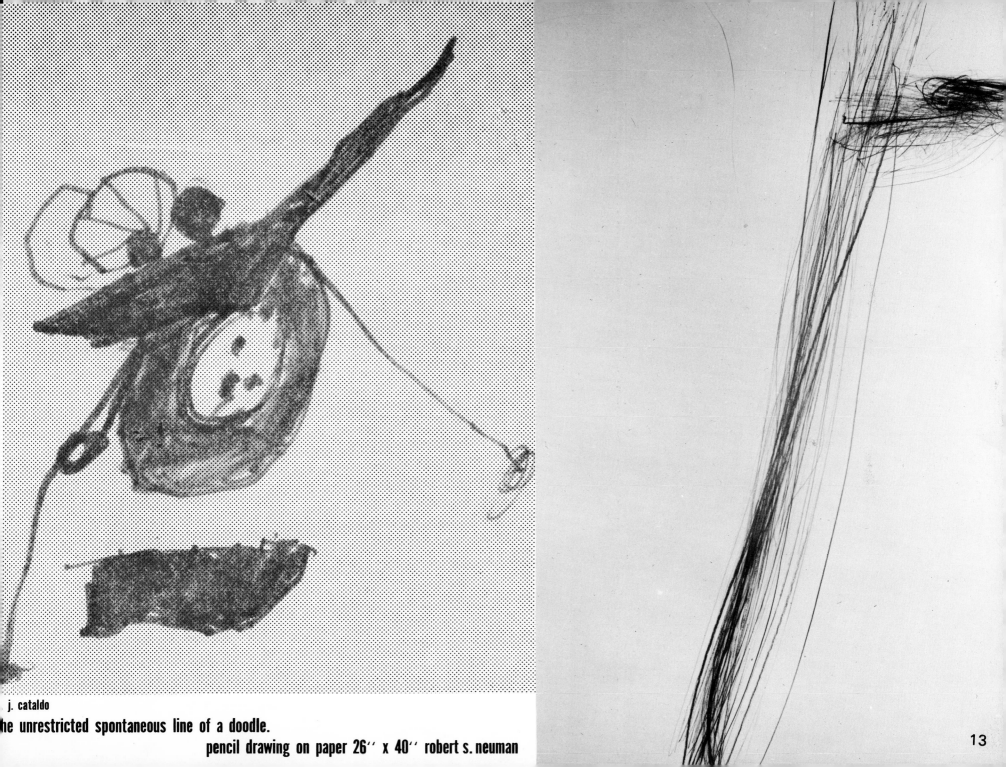

j. cataldo

he unrestricted spontaneous line of a doodle.

pencil drawing on paper 26″ x 40″ robert s. neuman

13

natural
writing

richard fraenkel

1.

THE CORE OF WRITING AND CALLIGRAPHY IS CONTAINED IN THE SPONTANEITY OF THE DOODLE.

/ an approach to calligraphy

calligraphic play with pens, quills and sticks.

after the calligraphic exercises with traditional and experimental tools, students could relate this calligraphic play with a spontaneous response to word symbols. as the instructor speaks words, students should respond instantly and without reflective thinking, using ink and chinese brushes.

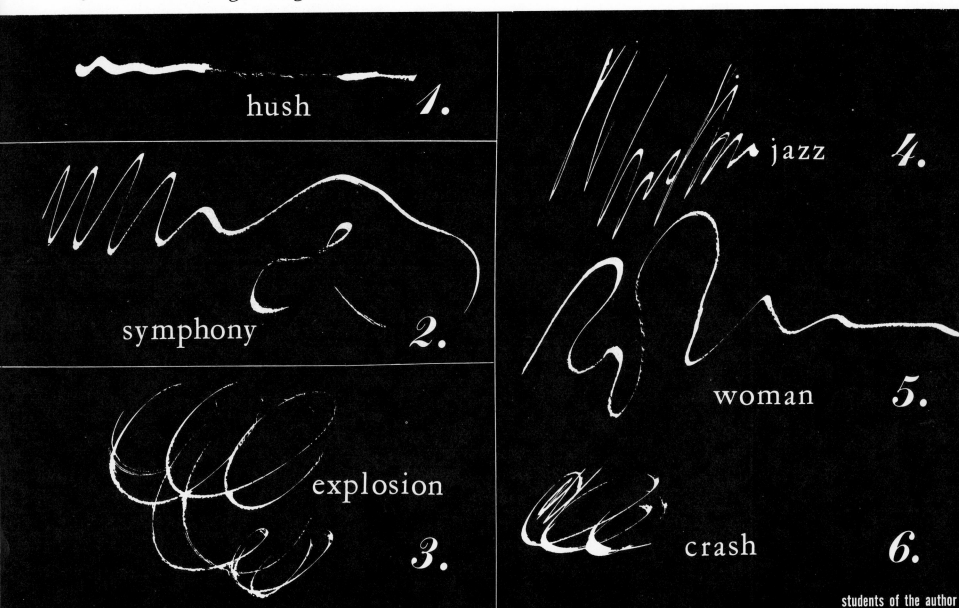

hush   *1.*

symphony   *2.*

explosion   *3.*

jazz   *4.*

woman   *5.*

crash   *6.*

as a next step take these unrehearsed lines and use them to spell out spoken words. this is quite difficult and many attempts have to be made until a suitable correlation is achieved between the mark and a word.

this unrehearsed line was instantly made upon hearing the word 'crash' spoken and this same line was used to construct the word 'crash.'

4.

brush calligraphy

"anger"/brush calligraphy

students of the author

a calligraphic ink drawing of "waves and rocks" by mort grossman.

this page shows how the student might proceed from a play activity with line, to a line that relates to letters with similar basic strokes. the approach to brush calligraphy has to be spontaneous and generally requires some practice work before the final job.

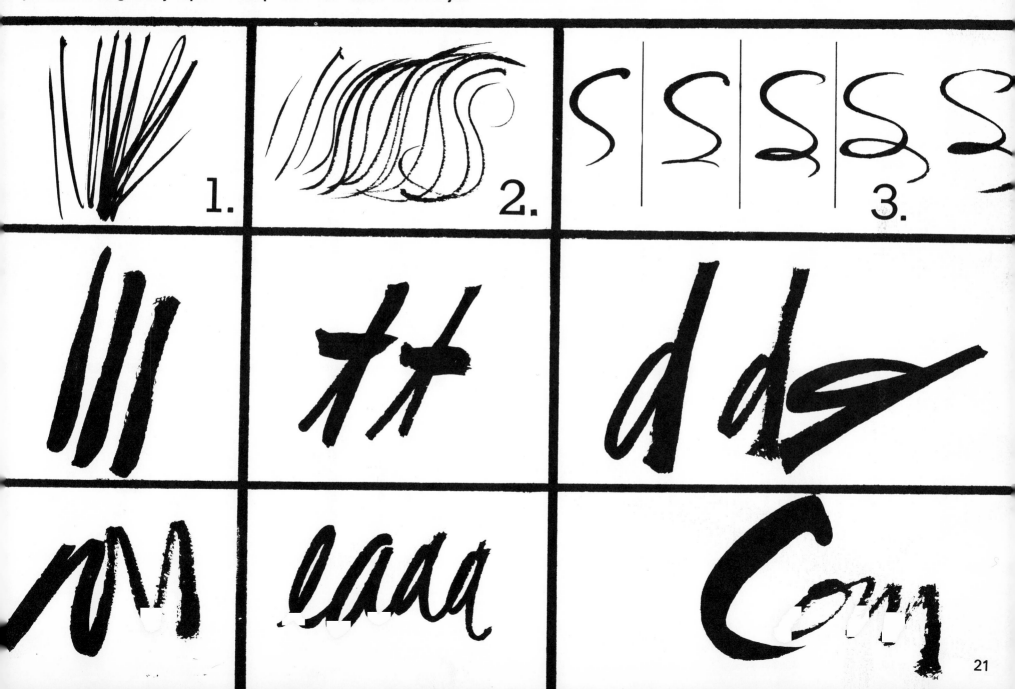

1.

2.

3.

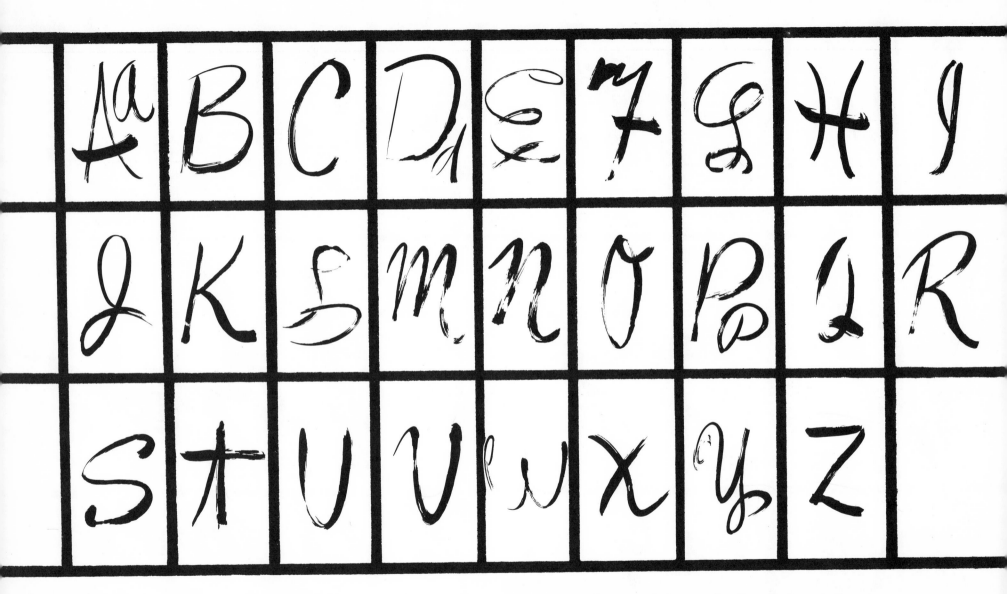

alphabet by clifton mc waid

a calligraphic alphabet of any merit must retain its spontaneity and flair.

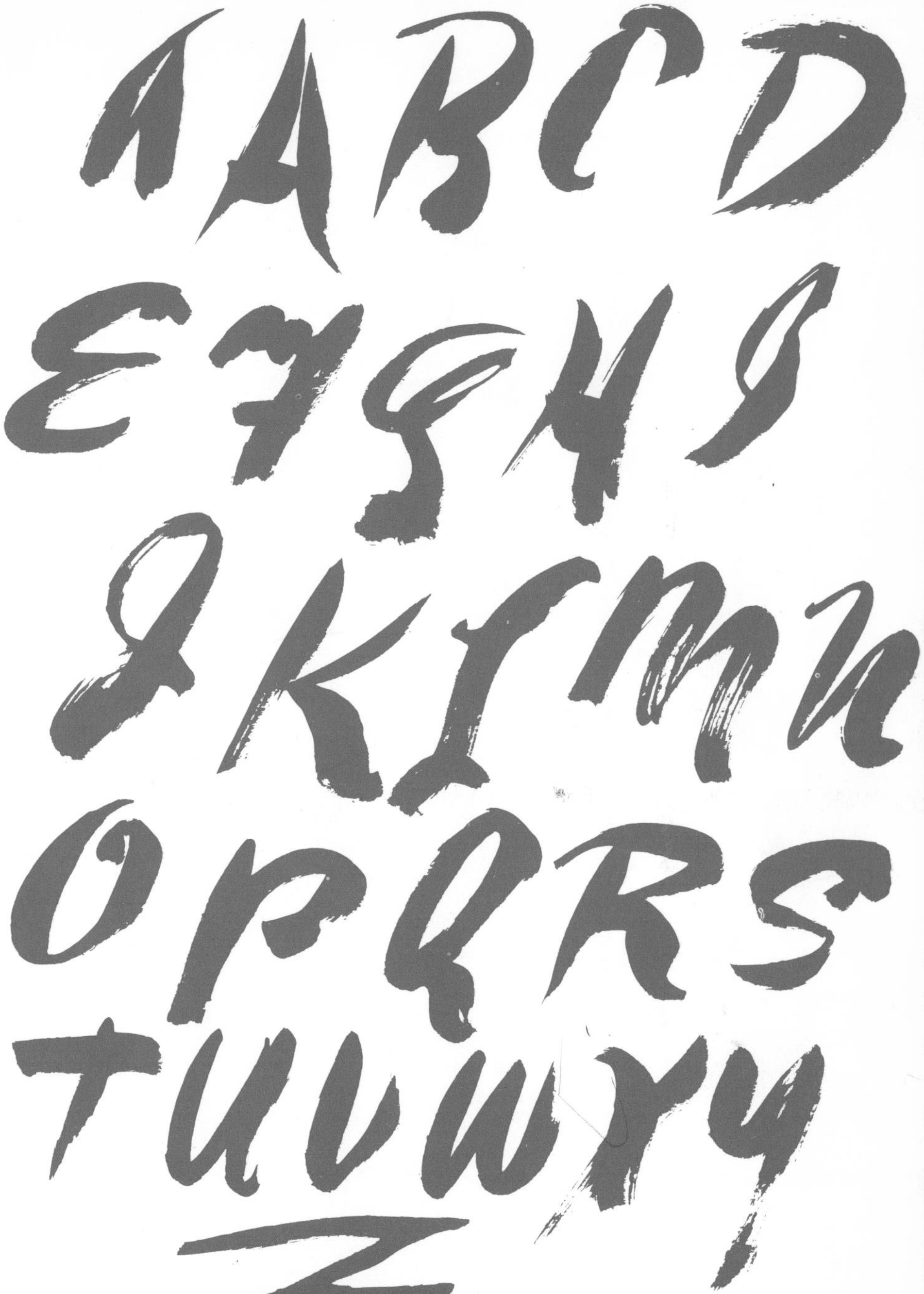

A B C D
E F G
H J K
L M N O
P Q R
S T U
W X Y Z

A A B C D
E F G H J
J K L M N
O P Q R S
T U V W X Y
Z

the above graphic plate reflects an attempt to solve a graphic problem requiring the inclusion of opposite emotions, concepts, or themes within the same configuration. some students chose to combine such basic emotions as "love & hate", or such basic concepts as "being & non-being", or such basic themes as "war & peace".

the poster to the right was accomplished by the silk-screen process. a liquid tusche was brushed directly on the silk and a glue resist was used for the printing. the student attempted to graphically interpret and enhance the literary theme and intention of the author.

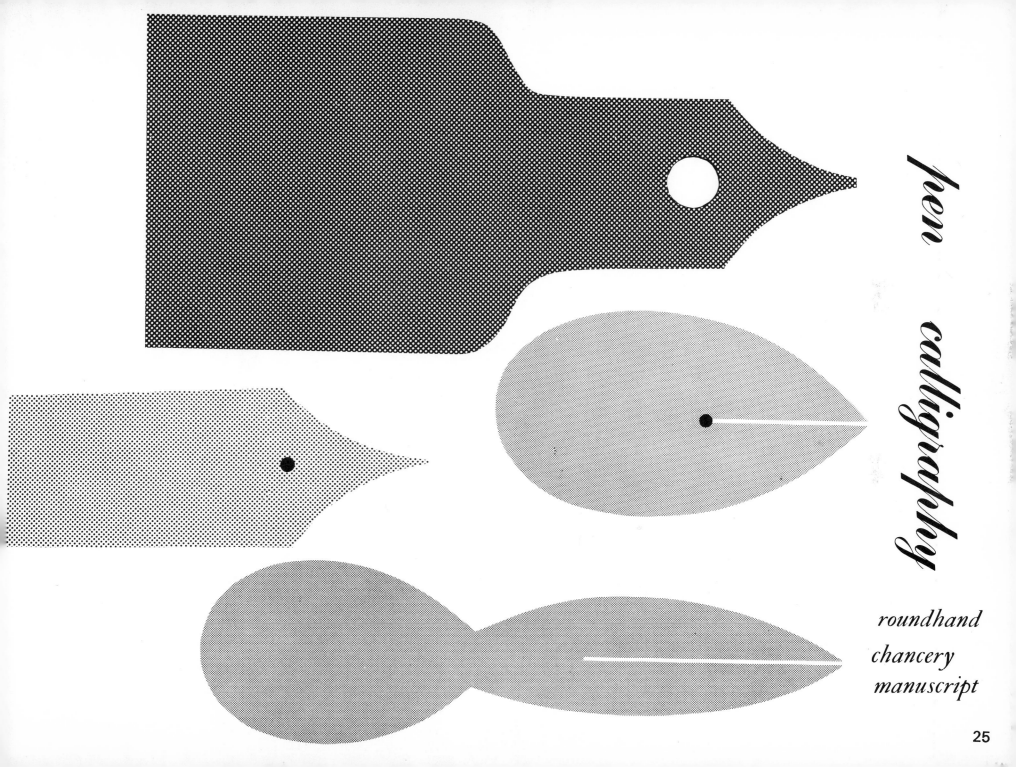

pen calligraphy

roundhand
chancery
manuscript

25

fatima ahmad/student/mass. college of art

PEN EXERCISES OF A SPONTANEOUS ORDER

the calligrapher holds the pen at a constant 45 degree angle.   the pen, after it is charged with ink, starts the letter stroke at 45 degrees, continues describing the letter form at 45 degrees and ends the letter at 45 degrees.   at no time should the beginner avoid this initial discipline.   the beginner should use the largest pen size comfortable to him.   the type of pen used for this alphabet is the chisel point pen with pen widths ranging from a near point to an inch in size.

SPONTANEOUS PEN EXERCISE USING A WIDE NIB PENPOINT

1 O
xyz
2
3 M Q

all strokes & letters made at 45° angle

THE "NAVAJO BLANKET" EXERCISE

because of the profuse and intricate geometrical patterns produced, this pen exercise is called the "navajo blanket". it is introduced as one of the initial exercises designed to reinforce the skill requirement of maintaining a 45° pen angle for the shaping of each of the twenty-six letters. the student is asked to saturate the page with the "navajo" motif so that he may gain command of the cut nib and pen angle while also controlling the open space of the page. a wide cut nib pen or a steelbrush is recommended so as to emphasize that the thinnest line possible is made on the unweighted upstroke of a 45° angle, and the thickest stroke possible is made by reversing the 45° angle and slightly weighting the downstroke.

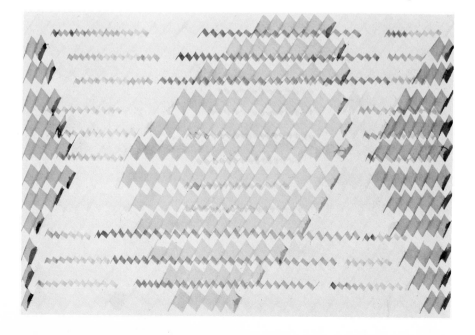

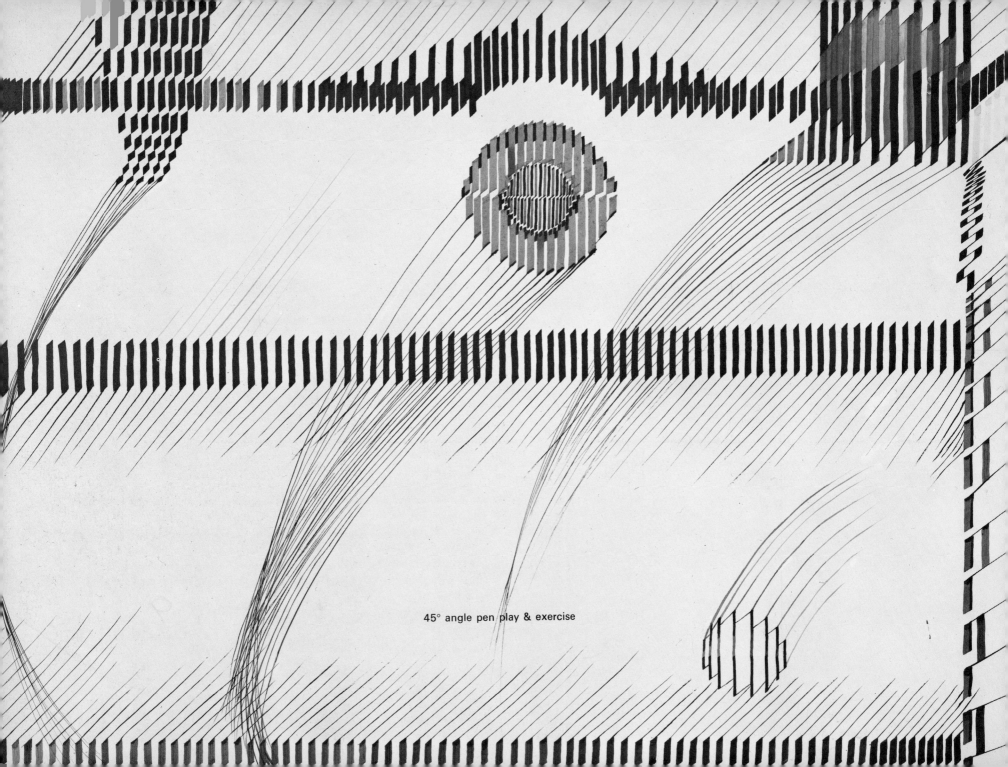

45° angle pen play & exercise

roundhand lettering by jane johnson

expressive calligraghy by j. lauriello

a round hand

Ecco

ego

5 | ecc eo

THE ROUNDHAND OR BOOKHAND WAS DEVELOPED AS A WRITING ALPHABET BY THE MONKS AND SCRIBES OF WESTERN EUROPE. ITS PRINCIPAL USE WAS IN MANUSCRIPT BOOKS. THIS ROUNDHAND ALPHABET IS ALSO KNOWN AS CAROLINGIAN MINUSCULES. IT WAS DEVELOPED AT THE TIME OF CHARLEMAGNE AND FURNISHED WESTERN CIVILIZATION WITH A SMALL LETTER PROTOTYPE FOR OUR PRESENT DAY LETTER SYMBOLS.

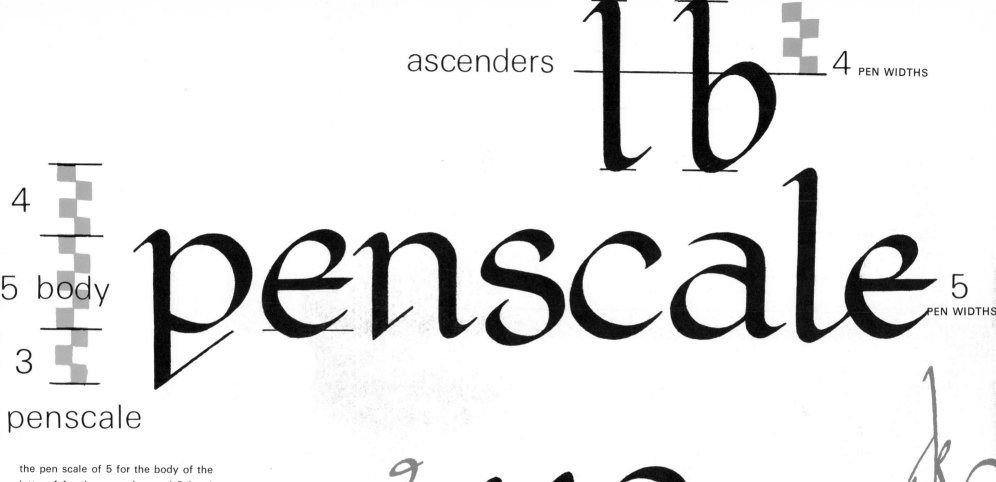

ascenders **tb** 4 PEN WIDTHS

4
5 body
3

penscale 5 PEN WIDTHS

penscale

the pen scale of 5 for the body of the letter, 4 for the ascenders and 3 for the descenders is preruled on the page very lightly with t-square and pencil. rule four lines: top of the ascenders, top of the body of the letter, bottom of the letter, and bottom of the descenders. add a space of about one quarter of an inch and rule a fifth line. this space between lines of calligraphy prevents crowding. remember that every stroke starts, continues and ends at a 45 degree angle.

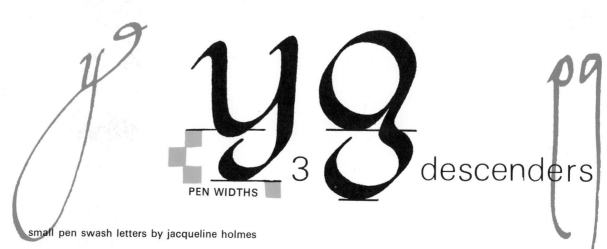

yg 3 descenders
PEN WIDTHS

small pen swash letters by jacqueline holmes

33

oce

the o, c, e are made in two strokes

A CLUSTER OF C'S

PEN EXERCISES

this alphabet is based on a circle. notice that the "o" is a part of many of the letters on this page. to determine the correctness of this basic letter see if a white circle is contained within the black strokes. many of the letters will contain one or two of the basic strokes of the letter "o." it literally is a roundhand alphabet.

e width of whichever enpoint the student is sing determines the letter oportion. one of the andard measures used calligraphers is 5 pen idths for the body of the tter, 4 pen widths for e ascenders or risers of e letter and 3 pen widths r the descenders of the tter. these proportions e only an average and e individual should feel ee to adjust them to his ersonal sense of rightness the letter form. index rds for the different pen zes save considerable ne when ruling a page guide lines.

ss ss one or three strokes sest qd

ss ss A CLUSTER OF S'S &

ss s vwxz4 ~

0233589~6.

36

Praise God from whom all blessings flow. Praise him all creatures here below. Praise him above, Ye heavenly hosts. Praise Father, Son, and Holy Ghost.

Amen

the student work on the left is a free calligraphic play yet it is contained in a precise form, while the example on the right is a sensitive controlled layout. even though both calligraphers worked from the same classic models, their results are unique. the sample on the left is a design using letters while the sample on the right is presenting an idea, using words that must be legible. many artists are inspired by the calligraphic form of letters yet we must remember that calligraphy is a writing process that requires clarity, reliability and precision in rendering; it is only by this precision that calligraphy can become expressive and aesthetic.

SACRED AND PROFANE
LOVE, OR THERE'S
NOTHING NEW UNDER
THE MOON EITHER

TOM MC SHERRY, CALLIGRAPHER.

C S D W

the roundhand upper case alphabet averages from six to twelve pen widths in height depending upon the pen style of the calligrapher and the nature of the job. the characteristics of the upper case alphabet are quite flexible and the calligrapher can make subtle changes in the letter forms. if the job requires using all capitals, the space between lines of type should be the same as the pen height of the letters. this will avoid a very dark page.

Z L i I F J K G

X Y M N T V B P R E A H

roundhand

chancery

a

A

a a

A A

a Chancery hand

the chancery cursive alphabet developed from the roundhand (rotunda) alphabet which was rendered by scribes at a slow and steady pace. by contrast, the chancery hand (c. 1400) was rendered at a faster pace, and consequently assumed the elongated, slanted and condensed characteristics of a writing hand.

ascenders

body

descenders

pen scale

the pen scale of the chancery alphabet is: 5 pen widths for the body of the letter, 5 pen widths for the ascenders of the letter and 5 pen widths for the descenders of the letter. the width of the pen point being used is the basic measuring unit of the letters of the chancery alphabet.

erosfiliusuyupe

agape-eros

PEN EXERCISE

agpe-eros

5

to capture the verve of the chancery alphabet the student should render letters in one continuous stroke. use a light body ink for easier pen movements and keep points clear by rinsing in a solution of a few drops of ammonia in water.

filias fo fluy
oldqq kk
juhnm

letter slant
80°

an 80° letter slant is recommended for beginners. it is an average slant
that may vary as much as 20° (60°–80°) with different calligraphers.

80°

the disciplines required to control the chancery hand are threefold: (1) a consistent pen slant, (2) the careful maintenance of one pen scale, particularly within the body of the letter, and (3) a consistent and increased hand pressure on all down strokes with a gradual release of pressure as the down stroke moves smoothly into the curved portion of the letter. with practice all three disciplines will simultaneously come into play.

44

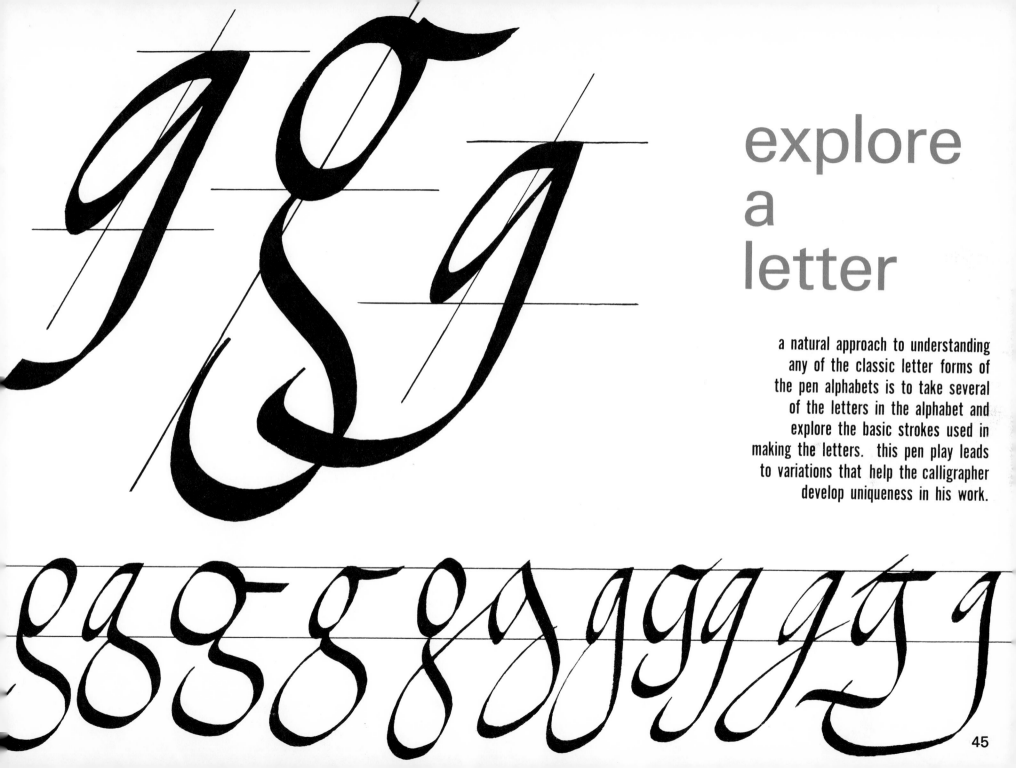

explore
a
letter

a natural approach to understanding
any of the classic letter forms of
the pen alphabets is to take several
of the letters in the alphabet and
explore the basic strokes used in
making the letters. this pen play leads
to variations that help the calligrapher
develop uniqueness in his work.

abcdefg
hijklmno
pqrstuv
w xyz
8Q tu
e y

CHANCERY EXERCISE

&

3 calligraphic hair ribbon pieces by m. stevenson

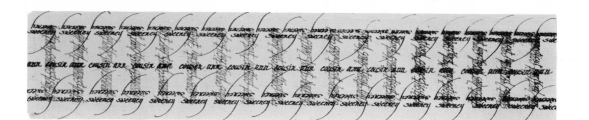

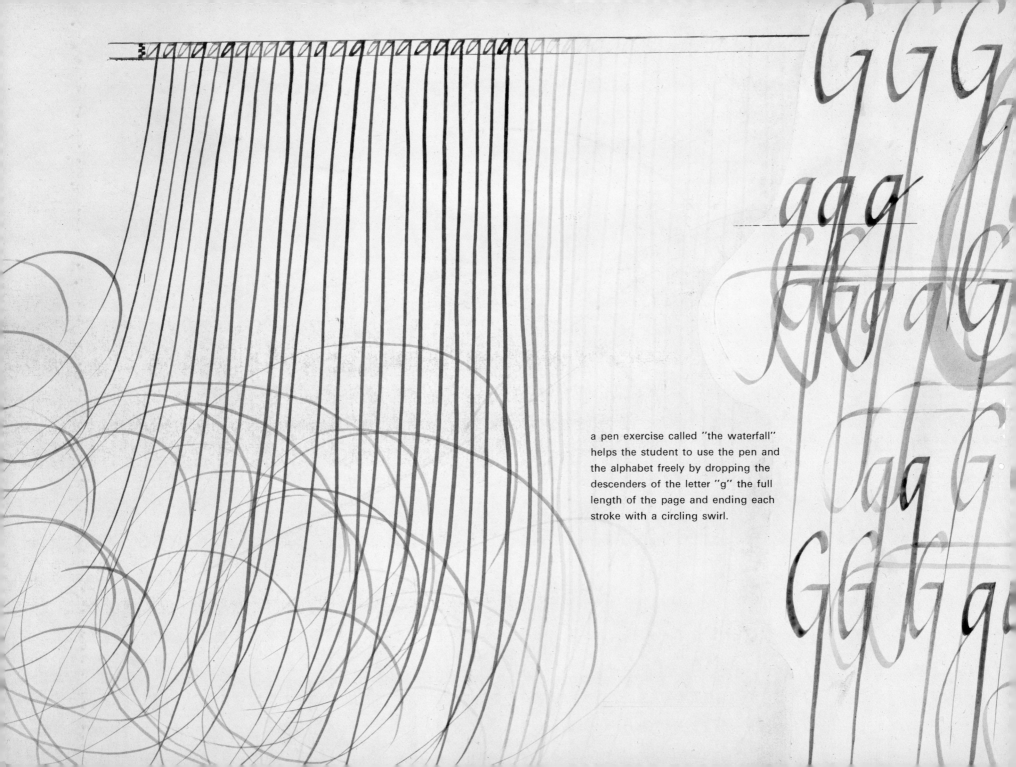

a pen exercise called "the waterfall" helps the student to use the pen and the alphabet freely by dropping the descenders of the letter "g" the full length of the page and ending each stroke with a circling swirl.

Summer thunder and lightning storms are
magic to my soul i dance with my
sister in the rain while my
mother puts her sneakers on and lies
still on her rubber matress but
lightning brings out madness in me

carol cartier

carol cartier

calligraphy by harvey chin

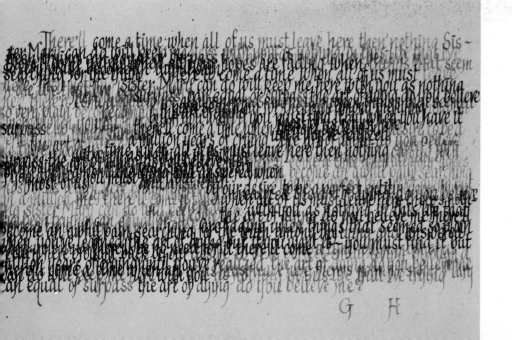

G H

back of the image, the few cords that bind
meaning in the winding
the rivering web
rises among wits and senses
gathering its own into its full cloth.
what does the worm work in his cocoon

when craft care elements,
the art shall never be free of that
that loom that lyre

the fire, the images, the voice

the threads twisted for strength

calligraphy by carol cartier

49

calligraphy by j. burgoyne

student lithograph

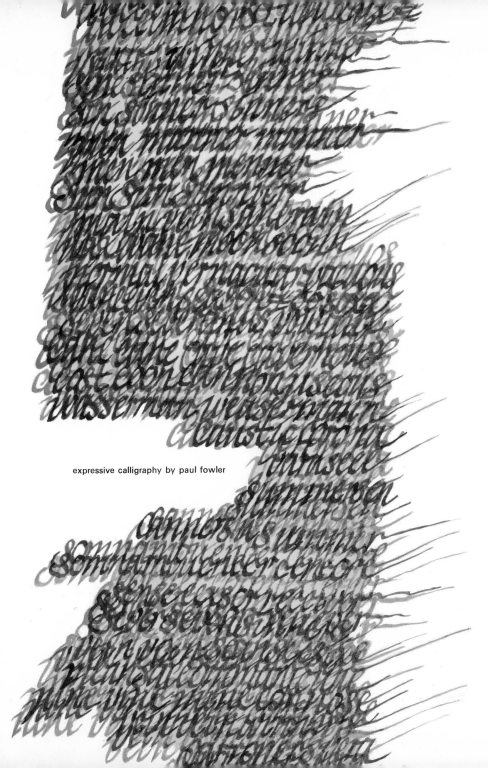

expressive calligraphy by paul fowler

gingerbread men

1 cup brown sugar
1 cup dark molasses
1 cup butter
1 teaspoon baking soda
dissolved in ½ cup water
1 teaspoon cinnamon
1 teaspoon ginger
½ teaspoon salt
4 cups flour

bring sugar, butter, and molasses to a boil in a large saucepan. add soda, spices, and lastly flour. work ingredients together to form dough. chill eight hours or overnight. roll out dough on a floured board (⅛ thick) cut with gingerbread man cutter. decorate with raisins. bake in preheated 350° oven twelve to eighteen minutes or until crisp and golden.

mulled wine

1 medium lemon
½ cup sugar
2 cups water
1 3" cinnamon stick
½ teaspoon whole cloves

cut and slice thinly ¼ of the lemon. place peel, sugar, cinnamon, cloves in saucepan and heat for about 15 minutes. when serving, heat 1 cup syrup to 3 cups red wine.

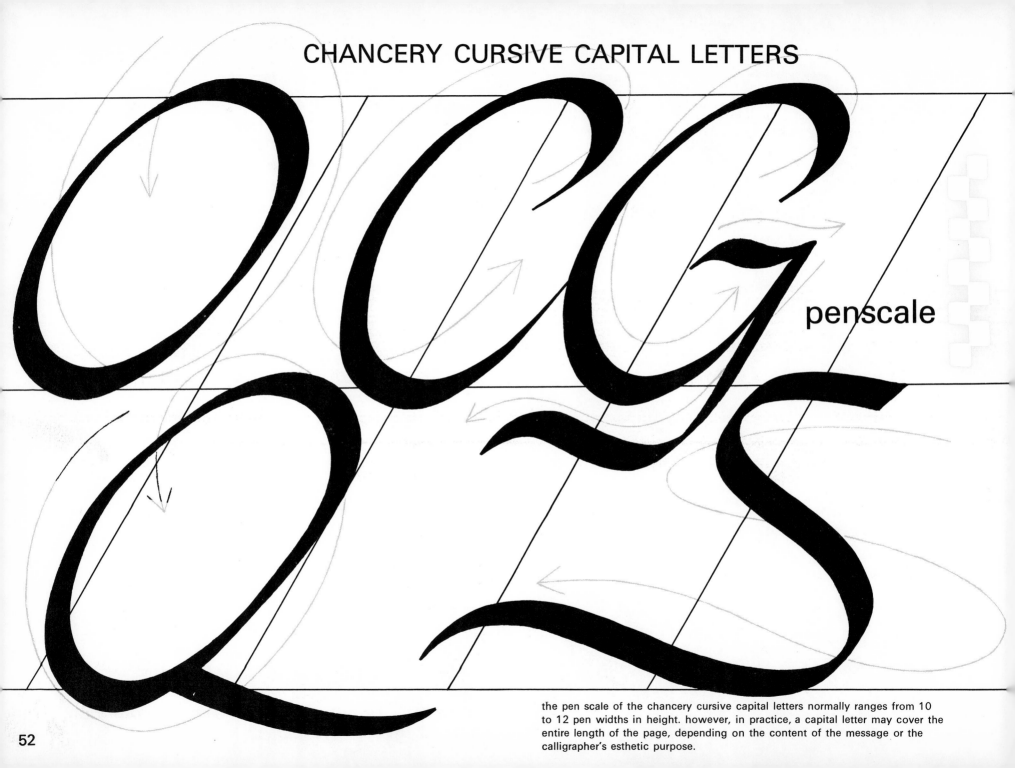

penscale

the pen scale of the chancery cursive capital letters normally ranges from 10 to 12 pen widths in height. however, in practice, a capital letter may cover the entire length of the page, depending on the content of the message or the calligrapher's esthetic purpose.

52

53

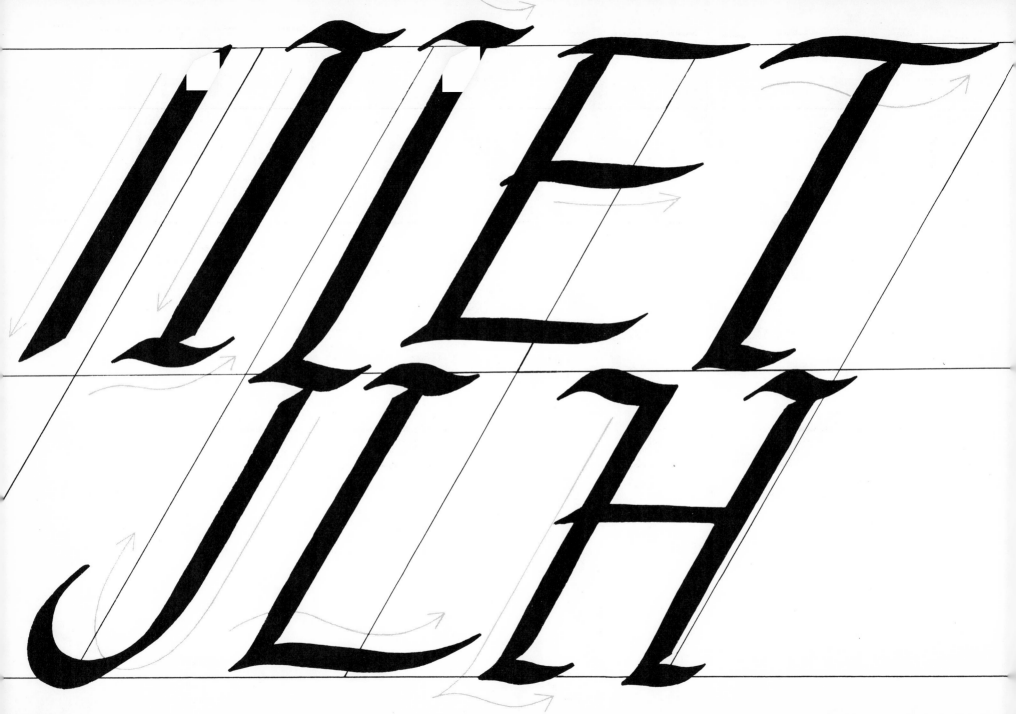

MAMBMCMDMEMFMGMHMIMJMKMLMNMOMPMQMR
SMTMUMVMWMXMYMZMAMBMCMDMEMFMGMHMIM
JMKMLMMMNMOMPMQMRMSMTMUMVMWMXMYMZMAMB
MCMDMEMFMGMHMIMJMKMLMMMNMOMPMQMRMSM
TMUMVMWMXMYMZMAMBMCMDMEMFMGMHMIMJMKM
LMMMNMOMPMQMRMSMTMUMVMWMXMYMZMAMBMCM
DMEMFMGMHMIMJMKMLMMMNMOMPMQMRMSMTMUM
VMWMXMYMZMAMBMCMDMEMFMGMHMIMJMKMLM
MMNMOMPMQMRMSMTMUMVMWMXMYMZMAMBMCM
DMEMFMGMHMIMJMKMLMMMNMOMPMQMRMSMTMUM

RICHARD HAUN

THE "M" NECKLACE ABOVE IS A STANDARD CALLIGRAPHIC EXERCISE FOR BEGINNING STUDENTS, ALTHOUGH MOST
PROFESSIONALS ALSO PRECEDE EACH JOB BY EXERCISING WITH AN "o" OR "m" LOWER CASE ALPHABET, OR BOTH. THE
TERM "NECKLACE" IS DERIVED FROM THE FACT THAT THE CONSECUTIVE LETTERS OF THE ALPHABET ARE PRECEDED
BY THE CONSISTENT USE OF ONE REPRESENTATIVE LETTER OF THAT ALPHABET. THIS APPROACH ALLOWS THE CALLIG-
RAPHER TO REFRESH HIS MEMORY AND TO ATTUNE HIS KINETIC RESPONSE TO THE STRUCTURE AND STYLE OF A
PARTICULAR ALPHABET. NOTICE THAT WHEN ALL CAPS ARE USED IN ONE JOB THAT THE SPACE BETWEEN LINES OF
COPY EQUALS THE OVER-ALL PEN HEIGHT OF THE ALPHABET USED.

Since i have set my lips to
your full cup my sweet
Since i my pallid face be
tween your hands have laid

Since i have known your
soul and all the bloom of it
And all the perfume rare
now buried in the shade

Your flying wings may smite but they can never spill
The cup fullfilled of love from which my lips are wet
My heart has far more love than you can frost to chill
My soul more love than you can make my heart forget
MORE STRONG THAN TIME   VICTOR HUGO

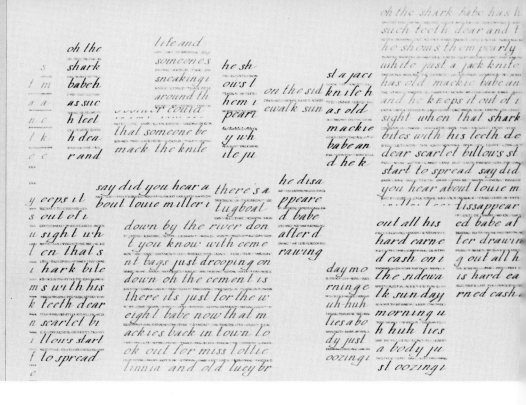

although the student is introduced early
to the precise and demanding skills of
the chancery cursive alphabet, he soon
reaches a point of expressive fluency and
abstraction in his work which parallels
a painterly approach to artistic problems.
his calligraphic images—even when
structured within architectonic formats—
operate in a personal symbolic dimension
which may appear to be far removed
from singular word meanings, but
constitute in their totality—an artistic
equivalent of the author's literary
intention.

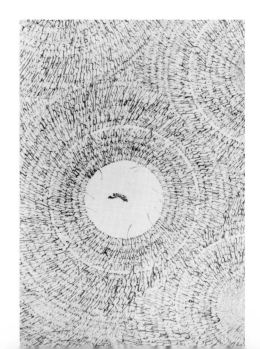

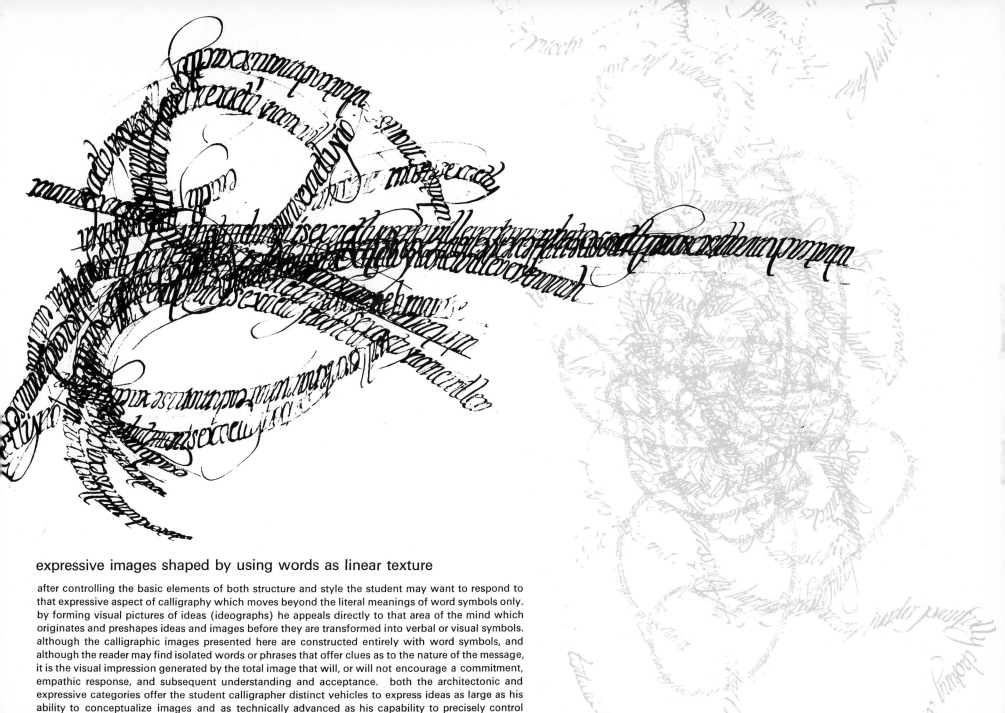

expressive images shaped by using words as linear texture

after controlling the basic elements of both structure and style the student may want to respond to that expressive aspect of calligraphy which moves beyond the literal meanings of word symbols only. by forming visual pictures of ideas (ideographs) he appeals directly to that area of the mind which originates and preshapes ideas and images before they are transformed into verbal or visual symbols. although the calligraphic images presented here are constructed entirely with word symbols, and although the reader may find isolated words or phrases that offer clues as to the nature of the message, it is the visual impression generated by the total image that will, or will not encourage a commitment, empathic response, and subsequent understanding and acceptance. both the architectonic and expressive categories offer the student calligrapher distinct vehicles to express ideas as large as his ability to conceptualize images and as technically advanced as his capability to precisely control the alphabet used.

57

Architecture is the art which
so disposes and adorns the
edifices raised by man for
whatsoever uses that the
sight of them contributes to
his mental health, power, and
pleasure

Architecture is the art which so disposes and

Architecture is the art which so disposes and adorns the

the student work shown here is an example of the quality of work done by students in the lettering and graphic design course of professor charles pollock at michigan state university. professor pollock describes the student examples as: "studies in rather precise forms ... involving the factors of space, shape and contour ... technique is confined primarily to development of an interest in and understanding of the methods most appropriate to the purpose."

CALLIGRAPHIC STUDY BY WILLIAM J. BROWN.

A fox was boasting to a cat one day about how clever he was. "Why I have a whole bag of tricks," he bragged. "For instance, I know of at least a hundred different ways of escaping my enemies, the dogs."

"How remarkable" said the cat. "As for me, I have only one trick, though I usually make it work. I wish you could teach me some of yours."

"Well, sometime when I have nothing to do," said the fox, I might teach you one or two

this sample shows how an expert calligrapher has adapted a natural writing hand from a calligraphic model, the chancery cursive. many calligraphers in their natural everyday writing hand use a cut fountain pen.

Assure that the distance from line to line of that which you write in this Chancery letter is not too great nor yet too little, but a satisfactory medium. The distance between words is that of an "n": between letter and letter when properly joined there is the amount of white showing between the two legs of the "n". But because it shall be nearly impossible to adhere slavishly to this rule, you shall be forced to take counsel of your eye and to satisfy it.

the child at a very early age is aware of the seemingly magical power of language symbols. he moves progressively from the use of letter and word symbols —that have no literal meaning in his pictures—to phonetic symbols rendered with a disciplined hand. the transmittance of traditional language symbols is an important educational goal, but no more emphasis should be placed on verbal communication than is afforded the area of symbolic invention within visual communication.

1

2

3

gaye 7 yrs.

1 2 3 4 5 6 7

4

barbara
age 11 yrs.

5

leigh
12 yrs.

l o l a b c d

6
6

O l G M P

6
6

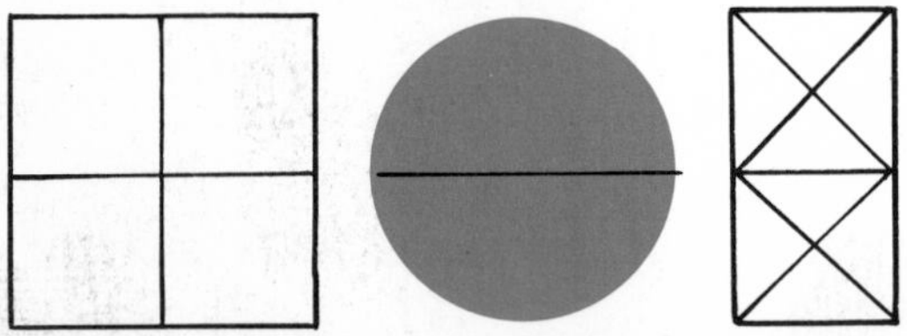

this alphabet can be reduced to a straight line, a circle and parts of a circle. because of its simplicity, it finds immediate use in the elementary grades as well as in the most advanced kinds of lettering uses.

manuscript

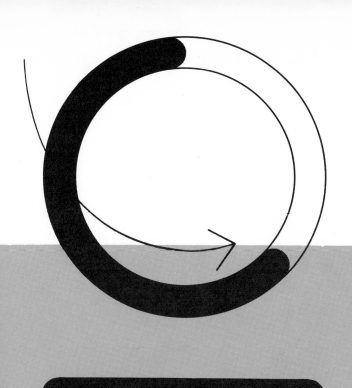

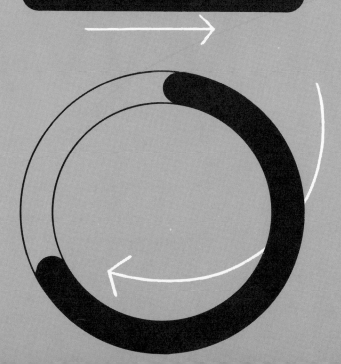

basic strokes

photograms / i. macdonald

the felt pen, chalk, ball-point pen, and pencil are excellent tools for this alphabet

basic letter shape

acebdqpg

tfumnhrjilvw

skyzx

pen scale

6

6

3

6

basic letter shape

the pen scale of this manuscript alphabet is 6 pen widths for the body of the letter, 6 pen widths for the ascenders of the letter and 3 pen widths for the descenders. notice that in the ruling of the page there is a quarter inch space between pen scales. ideal tools for this alphabet are the round nib pen, felt pen, crayon and soft pencil. this manuscript alphabet was made with a round nib pen.

manuscript

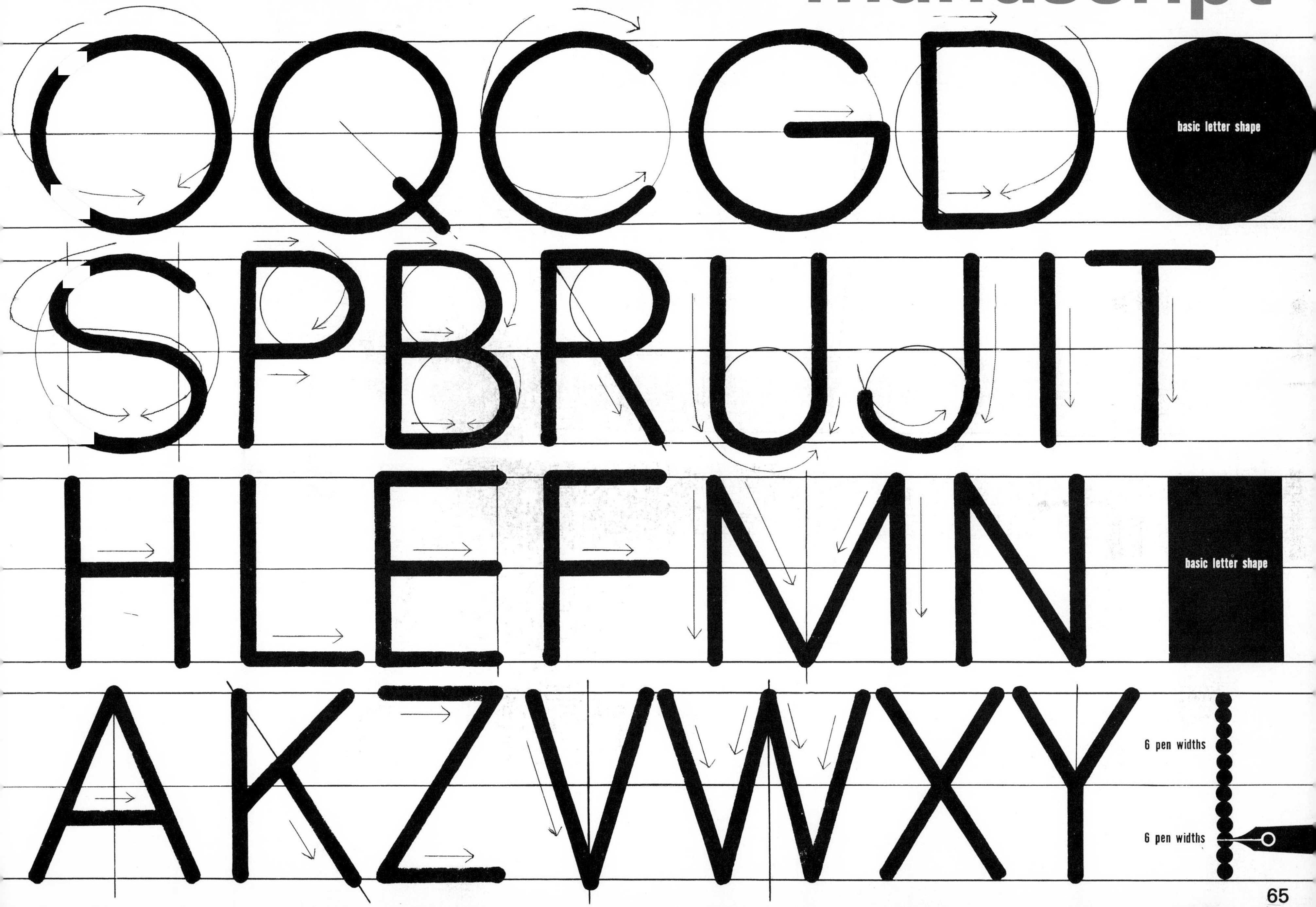
OQCGD
basic letter shape
SPBRUJIT
HLEFMN
basic letter shape
AKZVWXY
6 pen widths
6 pen widths

when the wind works against us
in the dark, and pelts with snow
the lower chamber window on the
east, and whispers with a sort
of stifled bark, the beast come
out - come out - it costs no inward
struggle not to go - ah no, count
our strength, two and a child -
those of us not asleep subdued

John D. Boyer
April 14, 64

when the wind works against us
in the dark, and pelts with snow
the lower chamber window on the
east, and whispers with a sort
of stifled bark, the beast, come
out – come out – it costs no inward
struggle not to go – ah no, count
our strength, two and a child –
those of us not asleep subdued

john d. boyer

the manuscript example at the top of the page demonstrates how one student
premeasured his copy by using a round-nibbed felt pen to rapidly letter the text.
this copyfitting technique discourages the student from pre-pencilling copy
and in a sense lettering the text twice, avoids the usual disappointment that
follows the inability of the beginning student to justify the right margins, and
provides additional experience with a new tool for shaping an informal manuscript hand distinct from the original.

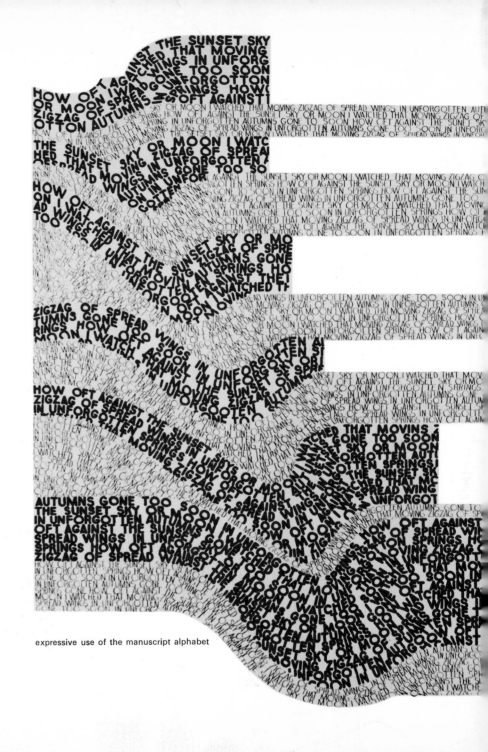

expressive use of the manuscript alphabet

phil runkle

virginia

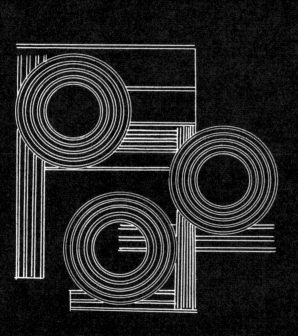

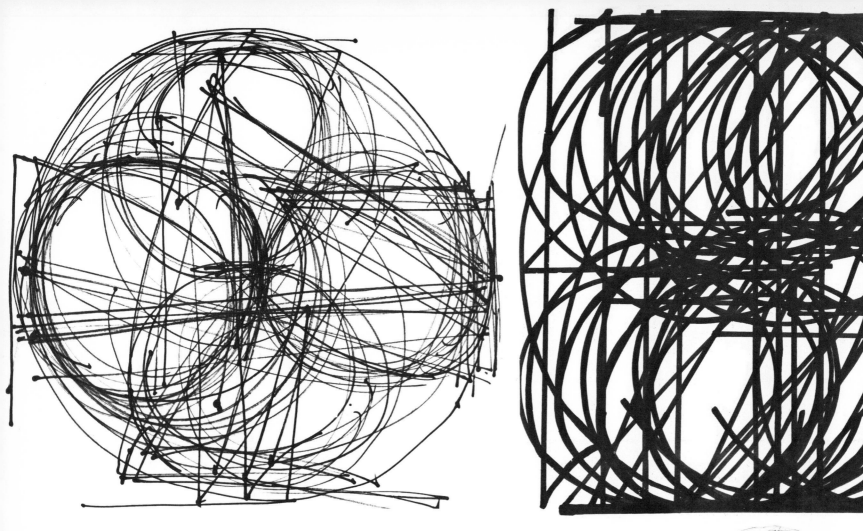

REFLECTIVE OF THE LITHOGRAPHIC SERIES BY JASPER JOHNS, THIS "0–10"
EXERCISE ENCOURAGES THE STUDENT TO CONSTRUCT MONUMENTAL NUM-
BERS IN AN EXPRESSIVE MANNER. USING A FELT PEN, THE COMPLETE PAGE
AND ALL OF THE NUMBERS FROM ZERO THROUGH TEN, THE STUDENTS CON-
TINUE TO OVERLAP SERIAL NUMBER SEQUENCES UNTIL THEY ARE SATISFIED
WITH THE OVERALL GRAPHIC IMAGE. COMBINING COLOR PENS ADDS DEEP
AND GLOWING TONES TO THE IMAGE.

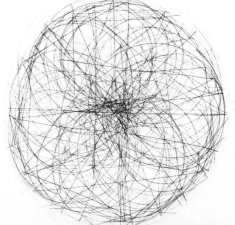

Mechanical Lettering

title page by George Yee

69

mechanical @lphabets

mechanical alphabets: g. yee and j. lockrow

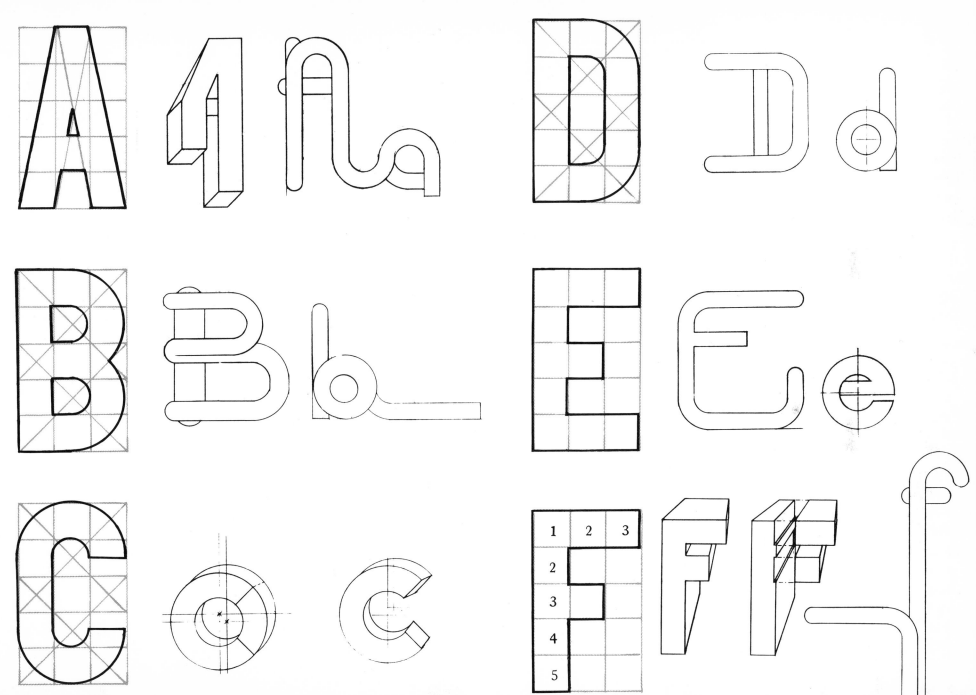

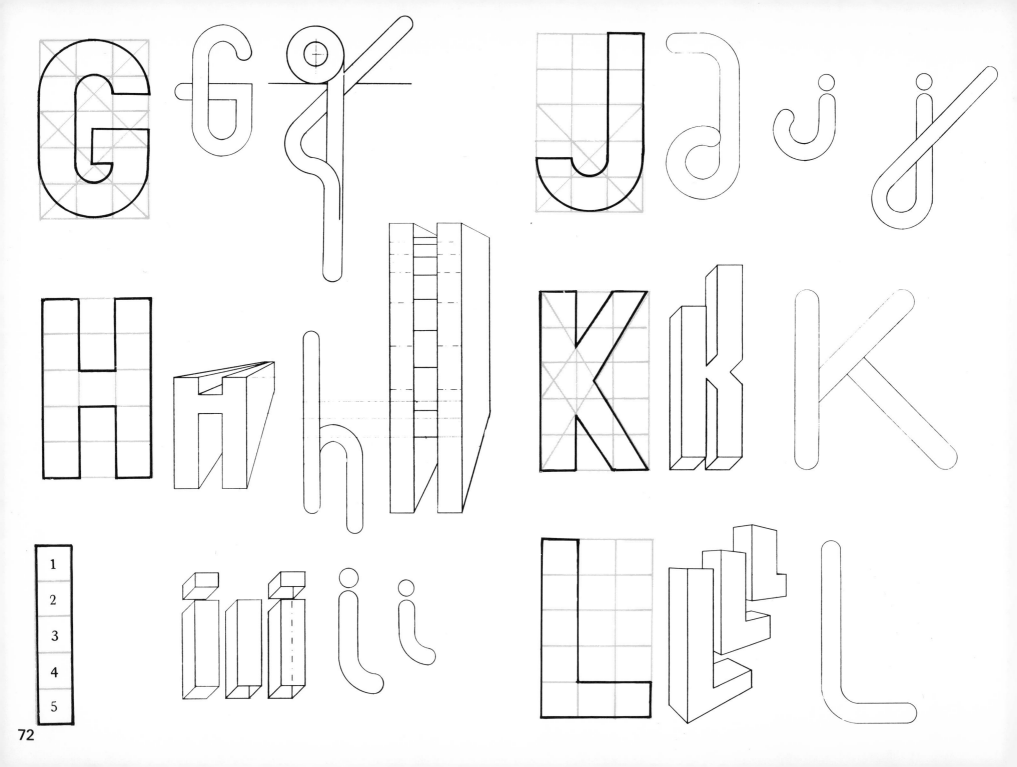

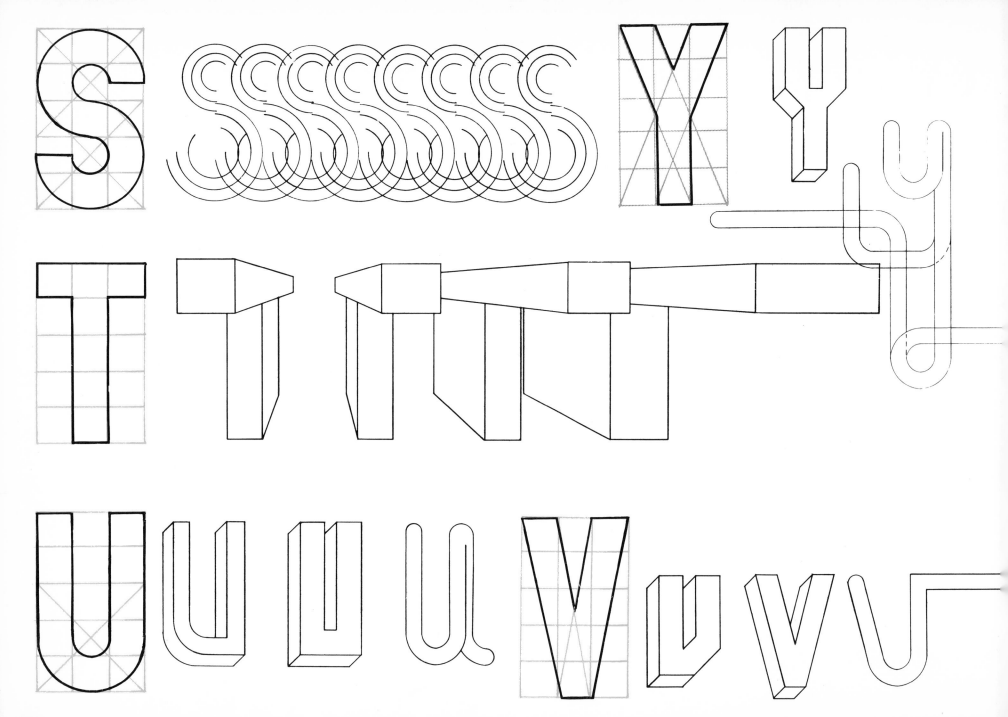

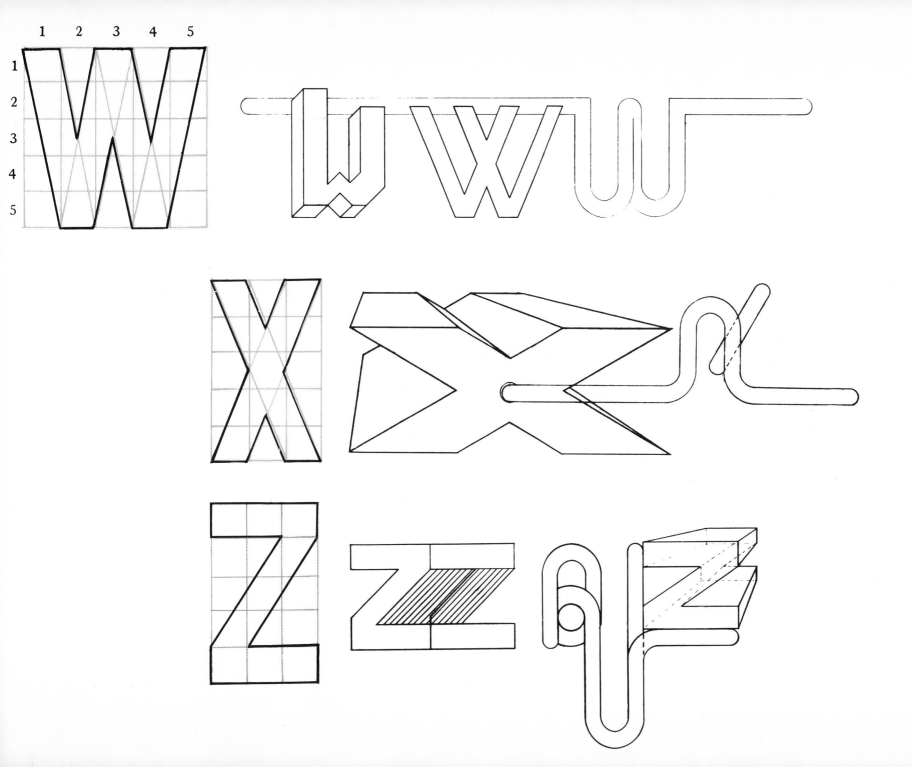

exhibition

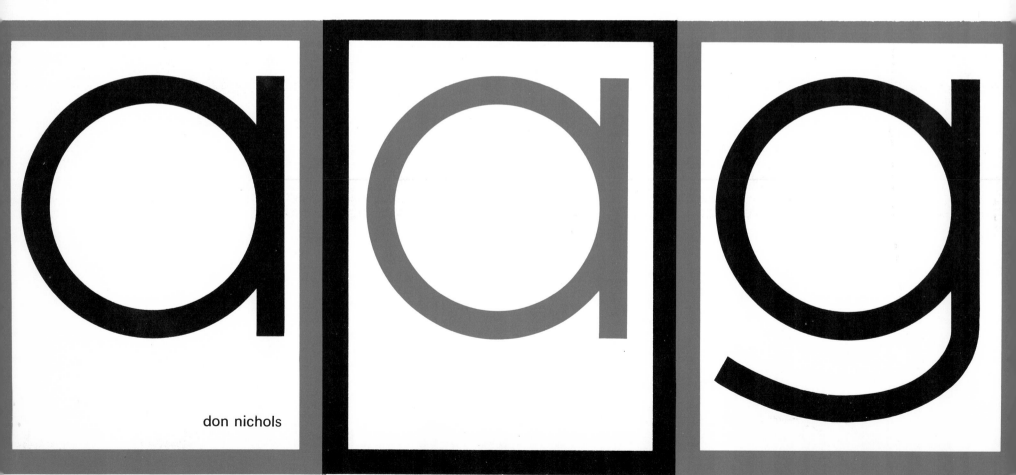

don nichols

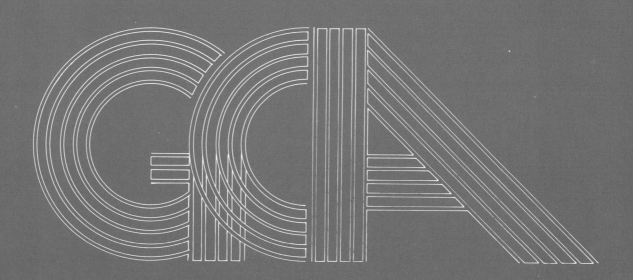

spiral

logotype designs by martha voutos

POSTERS

"to attract the eye and convey the full meaning in this visual turmoil of events, the image must possess, like the traffic sign, simplicity of elements and lucid forcefulness"   gyorgy kepes

national art education association

road sign by 8 yr. old child
quebec, canada

ZONE

Theater of the **Visual**
     directed by **Harris** and **Ros Barron**
presents its adaptation of

               Vasily Kandinsky's
               The Yellow Sound

Performances supported
       by the **New York Foundation**
for the Arts, Inc., with funds provided
     by the **New York State Council on the Arts**
ONE is affiliated with
the **Massachusetts College of Art**, Boston

The **Solomon R. Guggenheim Museum**
1071 Fifth Avenue, New York City
Opening **May 12**, 1972 for a limited run
Performances at **8:30** pm Tuesday—Sunday
Special benefit performance **May 11**, 1972
For ticket information call 212-369-5110

Kandinsky

poster design by malcolm greer

79

many rough sketches are made until one idea seems more effective than the rest.
these roughs are quickly made with the idea of exploring the widest range of possible
solutions to the visual problem. only one is selected for further development.

I

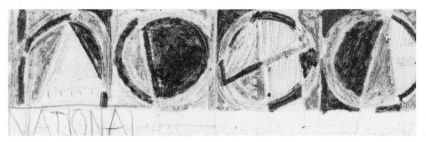

p. jedrzejek

a comprehensive layout is then made, in this case with cut paper. colored pencils, pastels or
tempera are also effective. the comprehensive should be close to the final solution with only
minor changes to follow; it is often used to sell the idea and make cost estimates if the job is
to be reproduced.

II

III

national art education association

A POSTER

1 alerts must be seen first before it can be read

2 informs implies simplicity & lucidity

appeals 3 esthetic correspondence

ethical implications **convinces 4**

&5 is lasting

implies that the poster effectively completed its communication task.

photography and mechanical lettering

indian

inks

b.punt

1 *hour felt pen posters*

*a more spontaneous approach to poster
design includes the presentation of a continuous series of graphic problems that
exercise the intuitive capabilities of students
and require a rapid graphic solution to one-
hour poster assignments. after three or four lessons
the time may be gradually reduced to 30 minutes
and held there for a few lessons, then 15 minutes
and held, then 10 minutes. less than 10 minutes
per poster seems to diminish both esthetic
effect and technical control and achievement.
using the felt pen immediately commits the student to
a definite stroke, while its expressive flexibility
removes excessive concern with
the technicalities of controlling sophisticated media.*

NEW
YORK

make a "me" poster

students may discover that after dedicated practice they have achieved control of the structure and style of an alphabet to a point of impressive calligraphic accomplishment. however even the most accomplished have difficulty in adjusting to the goals of poster design and seem to forget all their learnings when confronted with a first poster assignment. since the students have by this time developed pen and brush alphabets, it seems prudent to transfer this ability into a liberating poster approach. a "me" poster assignment usually meets with a smiling response at first, then slowly proceeds to wholehearted commitment and artistic involvement. making a graphic equivalent of "me" is no easy task for students, calligraphers, graphic designers, or painters. i suppose that only a survey of the total life's work of an artist might provide an accurate picture of his graphic attempts at self-realization.

a "yes" poster requires the student to shape an affirmative graphic image that is lucidly distinct from the negativism of the "no" poster.

the student of lettering soon discovers that letter symbols by themselves are not the most expressive way to communicate ideas. he discovers that certain conventional signs have a literal meaning that are readily understood by most people within the same culture. for example, the traffic stop sign, the arrow and hand pointing a direction, plus and minus signs, and many others. he also learns to use conventional trade symbols: the stripes of the barber pole, the three gold balls of the pawn shop, and any derivative picture symbol that represents a trade. a symbol represents an idea. it helps to make an idea clear by its essential simplicity and suggestiveness. for example, the heart carved on a tree containing initials is expressive and lucid, needing no verbal explanation. these communication devices are part of the designer's visual equipment and enable him to communicate ideas more efficiently and expressively.

signals

direction

exclamation

question

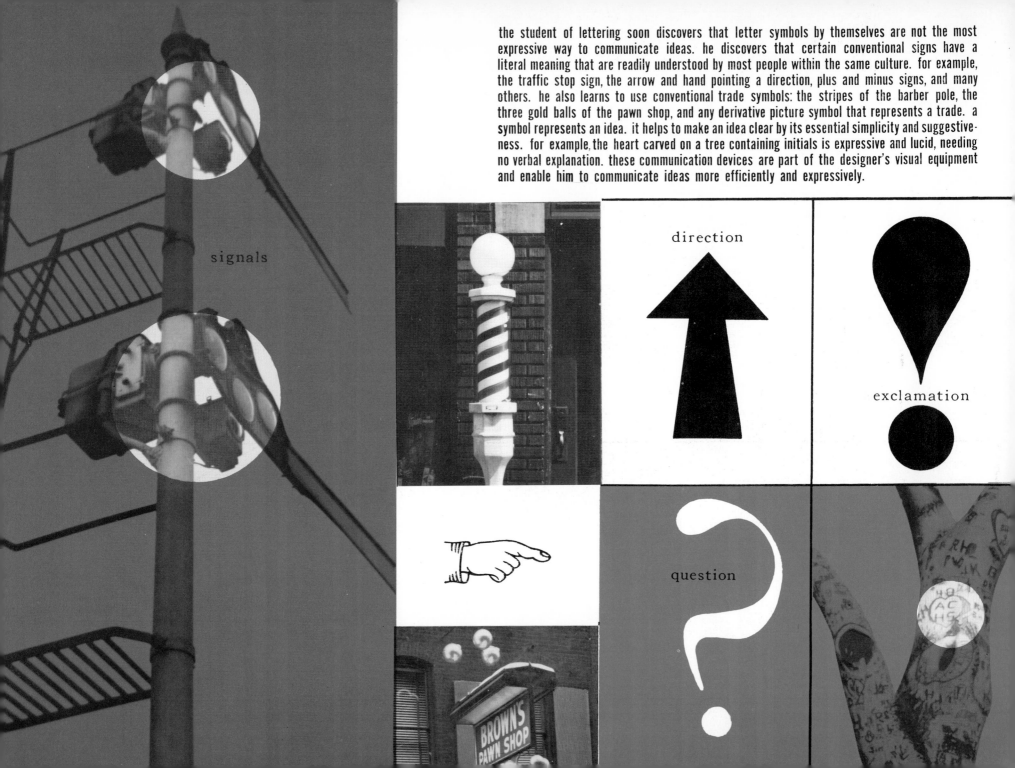

BROWN'S PAWN SHOP

the trade symbol

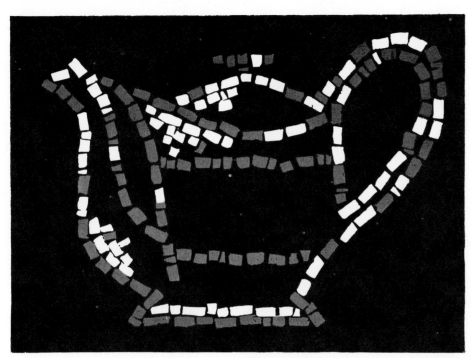

nichols

(ABOVE) A PICTURE-SYMBOL (PICTOGRAPH) DESCRIBING AN ANTIQUE PORCELAIN EXHIBITION. WORDS WERE ADDED ONLY TO DESCRIBE SPECIFICS OF TIME & PLACE. (BELOW) TRADE SYMBOLS (3D) DESCRIBING CLOCK & TEA SHOPS IN BOSTON.

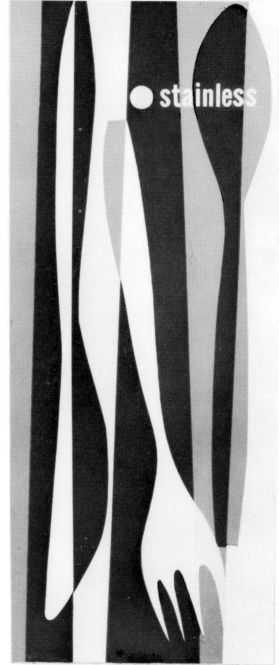

stainless

bassi

87

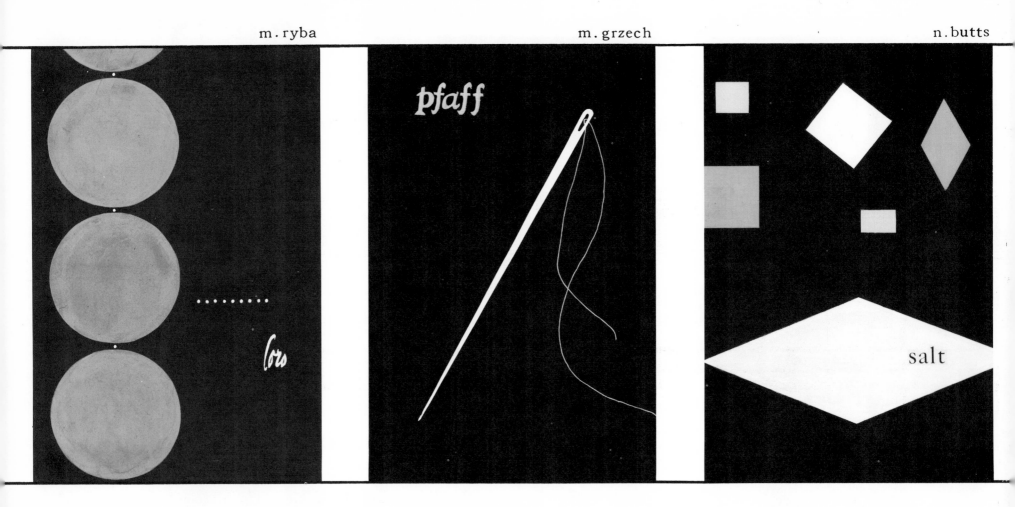

THE IMAGE AND THE SYMBOL ARE CLOSELY RELATED. THE

SYMBOLS USED ON THIS PAGE ARE SIMPLIFIED PICTURES OF

THE ACTUAL OBJECTS.

signs

direction

a directional sign of simplicity and clarity.

identification

a sign to identify property.

sales

a conglomeration of signs that confuse rather than clearly inform.

information

an almost unreadable sign containing a confusion of mixed alphabets.

89

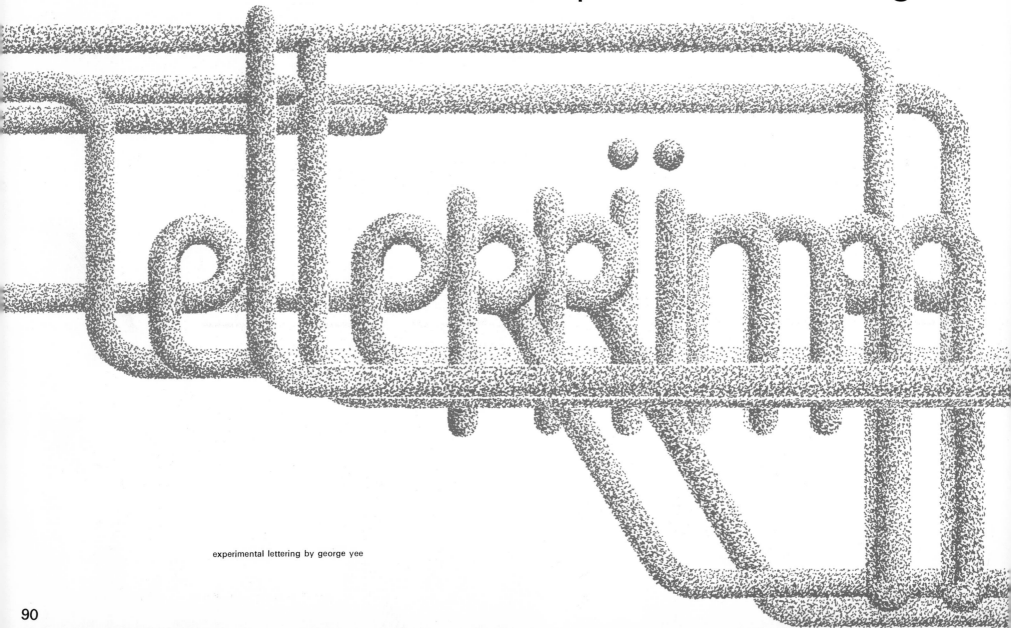

experimental lettering by george yee

pen & ink lettering by deborah deichler

GALLERY

woodcut lettering by connor everts

doodle a letter

one approach to experimental letter design starts with the use of a conventional type form. drawings and doodles are made which relate to the sample letter but begin to assume a uniqueness of their own. this kind of fun exercise can be done quickly and actually is a search for form. it is as stimulating as any game and the play approach seems to give excellent results. to the advanced lettering student it has all the excitement and profundity of a game of chess.

F. S. LAMB

examples shown are the work of students of charles pollock, professor of art at michigan state university. professor pollock describes these examples as, "studies in rather precise forms, whether type faces, letters based on early calligraphic models, or improvisations and simulated scripts.

LOIS JEAN SODERQUIST

ORNAMENTAL TITLE LETTER.

richard pynson

london / 1515

decorative letter designs by george o'connell

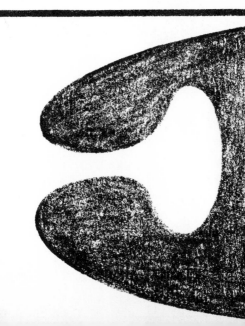

initials and decorative letters are almost always the natural result of a doodling approach. used in a page layout or poster they announce the attitude of the message to the reader long before he becomes involved with the verbal message. the initial letter can be a graphic image complete in itself, serving no other function than decoration or poetic imagery, or it can serve as part of a word.

charcoal drawing of the letter "k"

karen fischer

ball point pen drawing by the author

letter symbols are a constant source of inspiration for designers. letters and their elements have been used as design elements in a great many functional and decorative objects: printed cloth material, hooked rugs, jewelry and metalwork, and wood objects. the approach shown on this page is that of a student who is most interested in painting and uses the letter symbols for other than functional uses. here the student is making a design or graphic image from letters for aesthetic purposes only, he is not attempting to communicate an idea by using the letters as words.

STUDIES BY ROBERT WEIGAND

china

japan

egypt

persia

commercial calligraphy u.s.a.

the calligrapher although using phonetic letter symbols has attempted to show an attitude of conflict by using an expressive and descriptive line similar to that used by eastern cultures in their ideographs.

east & west

it is interesting to compare the letter or idea symbols of different cultures made with a similar tool. the alphabets of the east contain from 4000 to 6000 ideographs that are symbols of ideas, while the alphabet of the western cultures contains 26 phonetic letter symbols. the evolution of the development of our alphabet from ideograph to phonogram to the present phonetic alphabet was relatively easy to accomplish, whereas the eastern cultures are politically split on the use of ideographs versus a phonetic latinized alphabet. many eastern cultures have chosen to latinize their alphabets and are making rapid progress in this direction.

this page attempts to deal with ideas that concern the persistent improvement of handwritten communication by different cultures. the simplification of the ideographs of the eastern cultures and the phonetic systems of the western cultures seems to imply that perhaps a bridge between both cultures exists in the area of the so called phonetic shorthand systems and quite possibly a universal alphabet is slowly evolving.

ideas

pitman shorthand

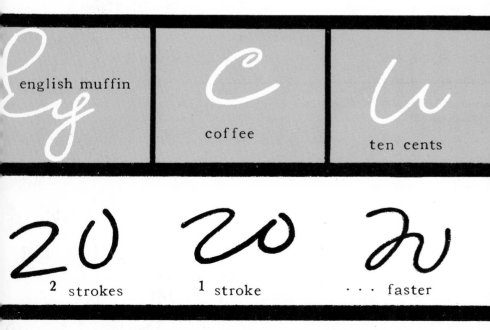

l itn ing

japan

the nakane system devised by nakane massayo is similar in appearance to the pitman system of english requiring a six months course for beginners to attain average speed of 220 symbols, not words, per minute. diet proceedings are taken phonetically and later transcribed for the permanent record.

r. k. hall

english muffin

coffee

ten cents

20   20   20

2 strokes   1 stroke   · · · faster

26 STROKES
歡
'joy'

6 STROKES.
欢

china: old & new ideographs

H. R. LIEBERMAN/CHINA'S LINGUISTIC REVOLUTION. N.Y. TIMES. JANUARY/1956.

the above examples of natural handwriting were made by a waitress writing out dinner checks with increasing speed. the effect of this increased speed was to change the form of the letters to a personal shorthand system.

chinese ideographs number about 40,000 although about 2,500 are in everyday use. to simplify handwriting an abbreviated free-styl writing is being encouraged. the next step from ideographic simplification is a romanized phonetic system. in existence in china is 28 letter alphabet known as "latinxua" which had appeal at one time. a latinxua association as well as an esperanto society was established in 1941. these tendencies on the part of eastern cultures to move toward phonetic systems commonly used by mos languages of the world are exciting to speculate upon when considering the development and use of a universal language.

ideas | abstract writing

literal treatment of an idea

literal treatment of an idea

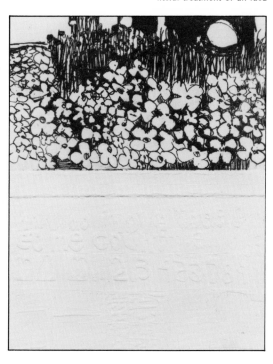

abstract writing has its roots in the traditional handwriting mode of a culture. as a point of departure, the calligrapher usually composes or copies a poem or statement that has a special or private meaning. then using a pen, brush, stick, the literal idea is developed into a highly subjective and non-verbal graphic image. the ''writing'' gradually takes on the characteristics of expressive painting and reflects the spontaneous departures made from classical themes by jazz musicians.

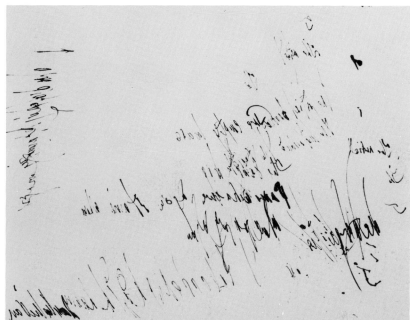

non-verbal abstract writing

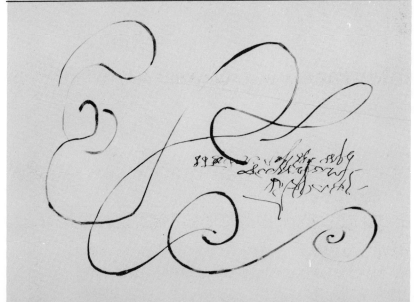

99

ideas | abstract writing

a calligraphic exercise that helps
the student to depart from a lineal
treatment of language and give a
shape or form to his thoughts is
one in which the literal information
is compacted in a graphic shape.
a graphic shape that ''looks like''
the thought, i. e., a graphic equivalent of the idea or experience
to be communicated.

calligraphic image by roma gal

many students, when developing graphic forms for their thoughts, design pictographs. they "draw" a picture of the idea while using the literary text as the shaping medium. curiously, young children, without cues or instruction, also exercise their expressive needs through pictographs. the phenomenon is unconscious and apparently universal and one in which the abstract symbols (i. e., languages) of all cultures are returned to their first source of image formation and storing.

sheila mann/pictograph based on the "journal of leonard cohen's father"

redesign the flag

students in an advanced graphic design class were given the problem of redesigning the flag of the united states of america. one student attempted to establish a graphic correspondence between the flag's design and the major crisis met and surmounted by this country since its inception. the single star symbolically embraces all the states while the large shapes reflect significant crisis such as the revolution, the civil war, two world wars and civil rights issues.

flag design/lettering and collage/gary barlow

any printed calendar may be enriched or modified in a colorful and structural manner by filling negative spaces and overlapping numbers with felt pens, ball point pens, or color pencils. the student may overlay the days in a recording and lineal order, or develop a personal calendar which moves as a series of color units from day to day, completing itself at the end of each month. in this student calendar each day is graphically resolved in a way that reflects the events of a particular day.

calendar by b. arseneau

ideas

the outlined lettering which carries the message, (in contrast to the compacted message), offers an intriguing correspondence to the reader. the message appears to be open and invitational, yet upon entering, the reader finds a maze of potential meanings. only by a patient unscrambling and fitting process can the reader reassemble the message as designed by the two student calligraphers. obviously there is a private and public dimension to language.

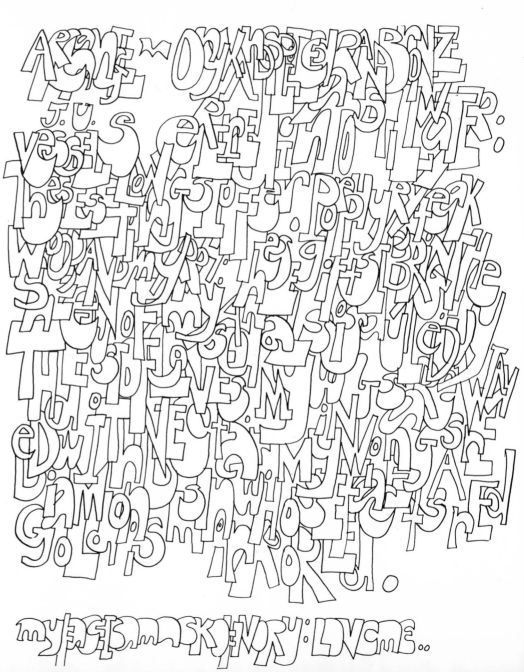

ideas

four student calligraphers, after achieving a high level of competence with their individualized calligraphic style and images, decided to work in a collaborative manner. one calligrapher would start the exercise with a personal thought, and the remaining three calligraphers would follow in a random yet serial order until the fourth calligrapher "completed" the calligraphic configuration.

the graphic outcomes of this collaborative process were unpredictable as was the choice of a medium by each calligrapher. at first, only quill pens were used, but later, pencil, graphite, ball point, felt pen, rapidograph and bamboo points came into play. eventually, the initial points of departure for each piece also varied from a line of calligraphy to an ink smudge, to a collage unit, to an infinite variety of elements including gold leaf.

ideas

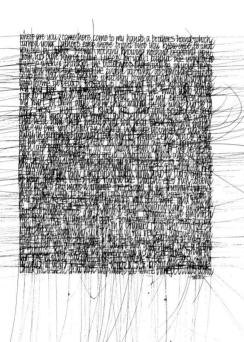

student calligraphers/massachusetts college of art

the technical requirements of the chancery hand
are very demanding and persist throughout the
varied levels of achievement. introducing liberating
exercises can advance the learning of those
students who may have become intimidated by
the unrelenting structural demands. the exercise
above encourages students to "toss off" the
descenders and endings of each letter or word
while using a pen point of narrow width. the
exercise on the right is called "the waterfall".
students carefully scribe the bowl of the letter "g"
and then carry the downstroke as long as the ink
or paper lasts, ending with an expressive circular
flourish.

he man sits on the curb his elbows resting on his knees, his head

DISCUSSION GROUP INCLUDED: ROLAND WISE/KEN WINEBRENNER/ THE AUTHOR/AND STAN CZURLES AS RECORDER.

IDEAS ON LETTERING BY 3 ART EDUCATORS

"i think that lettering is a separate visual graphic study in itself. i have broken it down into sections and started with calligraphy. we started with the idea of the doodle, then natural writing, pen and brush calligraphy, and then went into the mechanical letter."

"if they use a nib pen, they can't help but understand how lettering was structured. it seems to me that the ones who do some of the top work in the field do it without very fancy equipment. the ability to put down clearly and neatly what they want to say is most important. i would want to give them more reliance on the pen."

"there is always the problem of how to limit these things. you not only have the presentation of ideas, but you always have the level of ideas that we are concerned with. it is an idea of what density? they have to get an understanding of signs, of symbols. they have to select the tools and processes that will do the job most effectively for them. they have to make this selection even though the processes may be mechanical."

"in order to have communication we need to have the same signal system, and it is a little different from some of the other things they do in private art. in high school work, in many situations, the students, instead of getting the feel of lettering—the rhythmical feeling of lettering, draw around an outline or copy an alphabet card."

"i checked with mine to see what they were doing in other classes and i keep seeing that there is the same thing required as in this course, design. we are all working toward that. my students have done some fine work with their design instructors, studying relationships of different spaces. if they had more of that before they had layout i think they would see these relationships in advertising. at this stage we have to give them a great deal that will help them in design."

"i am glad the word 'precision' has been brought out. what happens is that when the students come here they live in dread of lettering. they are afraid of lettering because they are afraid of precision. they are interested more exclusively in the free arts, with no responsibility for specific, exact communication. in this course an idea, a presentation, is not good if it is not precise to something. it is all right to develop something in sketch, but then you must further develop and compose it into a meticulous form."

LETTERING IN THE ART EDUCATION CURRICULUM

I. *effective communication*

1. spatial control.
2. signs / symbols / images.
3. reproduction techniques and processes.

II. *research*

1. historical development of communication symbols and media.
2. new. developments in communication means and processes.
3. psychology of communication.

III. *presentation*

1. studio-workshop approach supplemented with lectures, visual aids, field trips.
2. discussion and evaluation related to individual problems.
3. class involvement with immediate active problems, e. g., school publications, displays and exhibitions, community improvement.

IV. *evaluation*

1. quality and effectiveness of solutions to communications problems.
2. philosophic understanding of the meaning of communication and effectiveness of media used.

ART EDUCATION DIVISION/S.U.N.Y./COLLEGE AT BUFFALO

ART EDUCATION DEPARTMENT/PENNSYLVANIA STATE UNIVERSITY
PHILADELPHIA COLLEGE OF ART/PHILADELPHIA, PENNA.
MASSACHUSETTS COLLEGE OF ART/BOSTON, MASSACHUSETTS

REFERENCES

writing and illuminating and lettering / edward johnston / pitman & sons / london, 1932.

the 26 letters / oscar ogg / thomas y. crowell co. / new york, 1948.

an illustrated history of writing and lettering / jan tschichold / a. zwemmer / london, 1946.

a book of scripts / alfred fairbank / penguin books, ltd. / middlesex, england, 1949.

lettering art in modern use / raymond a. ballinger / reinhold publ. co. / new york, 1952.

layout / raymond a. ballinger / reinhold publ. co. / new york, 1956.

cooper union art school publication number four / the cooper union art school / cooper square / new york 3, n.y.

language of vision / gyorgy kepes / paul theobald / chicago, 1944.

principles of gestalt psychology / kurt koffka / harcourt brace / new york, 1933.

vision in motion / l. moholy-nagy / paul theobald / chicago, 1947.

an approach to design / norman t. newton / addison wesley press / cambridge, mass., 1951.

gestalt psychology / wolfgang kohler / liveright publ. corp. / new york, 1947.

better handwriting / george l. thomson / puffin picture books / curwen press, ltd.

weathergrams/lloyd reynolds/1972

a personal statement

the purposes for studying calligraphy have changed and while young people
continue to opt for calligraphic studies in surprising numbers, their uses of
calligraphy relate to and reflect intimate and private happenings of their minds
and inner consciousness. young student calligraphers are less interested now in
transcribing the thoughts of distinguished poets and writers, than they are
concerned with a personal authorship of their calligraphic statements which
more and more describe a current psychological, emotional or intuitive status.
in an important way they are revealing a personal condition or observation to
themselves.
i have remained a fascinated witness to this self-unfolding process for some
two decades having had no idea in the beginning that lettering, calligraphy and
graphic images would prove to be a private joy, and that this commitment could
be so sustaining in those periods of great stress that mark all of our lives. perhaps
the ancient roots of language are deeply impressed and interconnected with
continuing and living human purposes.
students of calligraphy have ranged in my courses from ages five through sixty,
from the elementary through graduate degree programs. particularly rewarding
is the work i have done in institutes and workshops with public school art
teachers and children in the Dade County, West Palm Beach and Daytona public
schools in Florida, the Fine Arts Program (HEW) in Pennsylvania, the art
teachers of Portland, Oregon, the University of Northern Illinois and of Teachers
College, Columbia University.
the work of children is always uncontrived and filled with innovative surprises.
completely open to ideas, they may be sensitively introduced to the infinite
possibilities of spoken and written language while developing an understanding,
appreciation and high regard for the inner mind language they are constantly
exercising.

JnCataldo
9/30/74